Spared to Serve
Surprised at Every Turn

Oscar C. Baldemor
with Lynn Baldemor

Unless otherwise indicated, all Scripture quotations are taken from the Holy Bible, New International Version, Copyright © 1973, 1978, 1984 by International Bible Society. Used by Permission.

Spared to Serve

Copyright © 2023 by Oscar C. Baldemor

Published by:

WWW.CHARIS-PRESS.COM

Library of Congress Cataloging-in-Publication Data
Baldemor, Oscar C.
Spared to Serve
Includes bibliographical references
ISBN – 979-8-218-29745-9

First Edition: 2023.

Cover design: Celine Baldemor
Cover Image: Photo taken by Oscar C. Baldemor in 2018. This view of the author's hometown, Paete, Laguna, is from *Tatlong Krus* (Three Crosses) in the Sierra Madre Mountains, Laguna, Philippines.

All rights reserved. No part of this publication may be reproduced, stored in a retrieval system, or transmitted in any form or by any means-electronic, mechanical, digital, photocopy, recording, or any other-except for brief quotations in printed reviews, without the prior permission of the publisher.

*To **Ricardo B. Jumawan** or RBJ,
my friend and mentor, who believed in me
and wholeheartedly encouraged me every step
of the way. He was promoted to glory in 2021,
and I miss him terribly. How I wish I could have
written this book while he was still with us.*

*To my beloved co-worker and friend, **Jake Toews**,
who served with me for 12 years at CBAP.
He was a faithful servant and prayer partner.
We traveled together to many provinces
in the Philippines and shared many interesting
experiences in witnessing and church planting.
He has been in heaven for 15 years now.*

Table of Contents

Foreword

Acknowledgments

What Others Are Saying

Introduction

- Early Years 1
- First Exposure to the Gospel 5
- My Mother's Role 11
- A Girl With Long Hair 15
- Training Years 19
- One Summer 23
- Internship Year 27
- Campus Crusade for Christ Part 1 31
- Campus Crusade for Christ Part 2 41
- Through the Valley 47
- God Has Given 57
- CCBC, A Brief Interlude 61
- Operation 200 63
- The Camping Program 69
- Pastors' Family Camp 77
- The Role of Mass Media 81
- Travels 87
- Harvest 20,000 93

Move to the U.S.	97
Southern California	107
Going Back to School	119
Mission Trips	123
JARS	129
My Siblings	137
Our Growing Tribe	143
People Who Influenced Me	147
What Then?	153

Foreword

I am extremely privileged and grateful for the opportunity to write the Foreword of this book by Dr. Oscar C. Baldemor (OCB). His life and ministry have blessed countless people in the Philippines and in many countries around the world. He has also personally touched my life as God shaped and molded me from childhood to the present time to become His servant.

I have known *Kuya* (big brother) Oscar and *Ate* (big sister) Lynn since I was five years old in Santa Maria, Laguna, my birthplace.

As OCB narrated his first encounter with God through the ministries of American missionaries and Filipino workers in Eastern Laguna in the 50s, my father—the late Pastor Luis Pantoja, Sr., former town Mayor of Santa Maria—joined the same group to start the church planting work in our hometown. Santa Maria Evangelical Baptist Church became the first established congregation by the Conservative Baptist Foreign Mission Society (CBFMS) in 1955.

Growing up in the church, I had opportunities to attend the Conservative Baptist (CB) youth camps in Laguna.

Although I grew up in a pastor's home, it was during one of those camps, in 1972, where I received the Lord Jesus Christ. In the same camping program in 1975, the Lord spoke clearly to me, and I dedicated my life to serve the Lord in the ministry. I took a test offered at the same youth camp to avail of the CBAP-GIA (Grant-In-Aid) scholarship program for those who wanted to go to Bible school. In 1977, I entered FEBIAS College of Bible for my initial formal Bible school training.

During these years in the 70s, I became involved in Operation 200 (O-200) church planting efforts. O-200 was the vision of seeing 200 CB churches planted across the Philippines. OCB was the General Director (GD) of this historic movement. Since then, I have looked up to him as an inspiration for national church leadership. Led by OCB, one of the places that CBAP targeted for church planting was Manggahan, Pasig, where I served as youth leader, guitarist, and Bible study leader, assisting Pastor Joseph Jimenez, O-200 church planter. This was my first actual church planting training experience. Those initial lessons from O-200 gave me courage to accept challenges later to become Church Planting Director and Coach to denominational leaders for church multiplication.

In 1985, after finishing a degree in Sociology, the Lord led me to pursue a master's degree for more equipping in the ministry. Again, God used OCB and CBAP-GIA and other sponsors for me to avail of scholarships to enter Asian Theological Seminary. While my studies were fully supported financially, I had to find a way to support my wife and two small children. Again, God opened the door for me to work at CBAP. OCB took the risk of hiring me as Administrative Assistant (a better name for driver-messenger) and to coordinate a Bible distribution project called Project Philip. I did not tell OCB that my driving experience was only two years. Thank God for His protection as I drove the CBAP GD and Mr. Jake Toews (Conservative Baptist Missions missionary and CBAP Church Planting Director) to Baguio, Nueva Vizcaya, Dagupan, etc. for ministry. Being with OCB and many CB leaders, including the Simons, Carveys, Davises, Roger Baldemor, Nanding Alconga, Tony Pezzota, Fred Magbanua, and many other spiritual giants who became my mentors in life and ministry, were equally important learning opportunities along with my seminary training.

OCB and Ate Lynn also led CBAP in evangelistic film production. It was a wonderful experience for me to be in a lead role alongside veteran actress Miss Rosa Rosal in a Holy Week TV drama shown in four major Philippine networks.

When I started my pastoral ministry in the late 80s and the 90s, OCB led teams from Fil-Am Christian Fellowship in Long Beach and other American churches to help in evangelistic campaigns in the Philippines. I was pastor at Evangel Baptist Church Paranaque during this time. We hosted their teams as volunteers went to the streets of Pildera and Santo Niño in Paranaque. This led to the planting of a new church in the area.

Our relationship and friendship continued during my 10-year ministry stint in the Washington DC area. OCB and family graciously hosted me in their Lakewood home, and even took me on a short trip to Palm Springs, California.

In 2005, the Lord led Jeni and me to complete our ministry in the Washington DC area, and to serve at CBAP, our home church association, as new General Director. It was a humbling, indescribable experience as a former messenger-driver, becoming the GD and CEO of CBAP! I learned that the search team consulted OCB and he gave a recommendation to consider me as one of the candidates. I served as the fourth CBAP GD from 2005-2015 after Rev. Rene Atienza's fruitful leadership. It was also CBAP's 50th Anniversary where they evaluated 50 years of the association's ministry and charted the course for the next 10 years.

From there, our ministry partnership continued through a series of CBF and Fil-Am churches' short medical mission trips in Laoag, Bataan, Negros province, and Zambales that led to the establishment of new churches. During this time, OCB also founded JARS Ministries that sponsored many pastors' kids (PK) in their college education. Scores of PKs are now professionals and are making economic progress in their lives.

From a youth leader, an aspiring pastor, CBAP worker, young pastor-teacher-church planter, to PCEC director and CEO uniting 87 denominations, 55,000 churches for the discipleship of the Philippines, I look back and give glory to God for the life of OCB whom God has used to help shape and mold my life through his ministry, influence, and support.

I praise God for this book that honors God. OCB has walked with God, served in various ministries locally and globally, and is still running the race strongly with his vision of serving seniors and seasoned workers for enrichment, encouragement, and rest. This memoir will inspire many to follow and serve God faithfully, run the race well, and be strong until the race is finished.

Bishop Noel Pantoja
National Director and CEO
Philippine Council of Evangelical Churches

Acknowledgments

I wish to acknowledge my wife Lynn for her support and encouragement, for typing the manuscript, proofreading, and editing. I also requested her to write two chapters about our family.

Special thanks to my eldest daughter Celine for designing the front and back covers, proofreading, and doing the layout.

I also thank Rev. Aubrey "Bo" Horlen, Dr. Frank Pardue and my daughter Lynette for reading the manuscript and making helpful suggestions and corrections.

I acknowledge the CBAP office personnel for allowing me to dig into their archives.

I thank Flor Pangga, Dr. Russell Atonson, and Normi Garcia-Panuncialman for sharing detailed information that I included in this book.

Thanks, also, to Pastor Jerry Olarte, Mrs. Chit Alcantara-Lascano, and Pastor Dan Bautista for sharing their camping testimonies.

I must acknowledge Dr. John Redman and Charis Press for publishing this book and for giving generous help beyond all expectations.

Special thanks to Bishop Noel Pantoja for writing the Foreword. I also thank those who graciously shared their endorsements.

Above all, I'm grateful to God for giving me physical strength, clarity of mind, and spiritual insight in the writing of this memoir. TO HIM ALONE BE THE GLORY!

What Others Are Saying

Dr. Oscar Baldemor was my director and trainer when I joined the staff training of Cru in 1974-75. There were only a few people I looked up to then and Kuya Oscar was one of them. His heart for ministry and his presence in the campus where I was assigned, his giving directions, and his leading the staff in evangelism and discipleship were evident. I admired his speaking ability and boldness. He also pushed me to do the same, like doing mass evangelism in the dormitories and classrooms.

I am glad that he has written this memoir. His stories help not only in bringing back good memories but also in serving as examples to the present and future generations of what God can do when we commit our lives to Him.

Dr. Teody Pajaron
Cru Staff Emeritus
Chairman, Board of Trustees
FamilyLife Philippines

In his memoir, Dr. Oscar Baldemor proves that God has prepared and used him through his various involvements with churches and organizations. God's hand is clearly seen all throughout the pages of this memoir. This book speaks strongly about courage, endurance, determination, and perseverance—which I believe a true servant of God must possess.

Dr. Reynaldo Avante
General Director
CB Association of the Philippines

Kudos to Oscar Baldemor for being a significant person during my Campus Crusade days at the University of the Philippines (UP). Oscar has always been a prime mover. He introduced me to Greenhills Christian Fellowship and to Pastor Luis Pantoja, Jr. He also introduced me to my partner in life, Pastor Mike Lacanilao. This book will be a very good read for those who desire to be in Christian ministry, both in the campus and in the church community.

Teacher Francie Castañeda-Lacanilao
Founder and Director
The Learning Tree, Philippines

Dr. Oscar Baldemor was used by our Lord in key leadership positions both in Campus Crusade and the Conservative Baptist Association of the Philippines as God initiated a movement of His Spirit to bring millions of Filipinos to faith in and obedience to Christ. Dr. Baldemor's memoir gives us poignant reminders of what Jesus did and how he did it in the key decades of the 20th century as this Spirit-led movement gathered momentum. This book is written in a pithy and action-packed style and is well worth reading. Peter wrote his final letter to the 1st century Church for a similar purpose according to 2 Peter 1:13-15:

> [13] *I think it right, if I am in this body, to stir you up by way of reminder,* [14] *since I know that the putting off of my body will be soon, as our Lord Jesus Christ made clear to me.* [15] *And I will make every effort so that after my departure you may be able at any time to recall these things.* (ESV)

Rev. Aubrey "Bo" Horlen
Former WorldVenture Missionary to the Philippines

I am thankful for the chance to recommend this book to you! Oscar and Lynn were key people during a key time for evangelicals in the Philippines and their story needs to be heard. Not enough of us know all that went into what we could call the Philippines' "Jesus Revolution"—pre-"People Power" days. They served during the early years of Cru, CBAP, and PCEC—all great organizations that helped shape the Christian Church throughout the country. They also formed our ministry trajectory as well. *Salamat sa Ginoo!!!*

Dr. Frank Pardue
Director Emeritus
DMin in Transformational Leadership
International Graduate School of Leadership
Philippines

The first time I met Dr. Oscar Baldemor was in 2005, when he visited our church, Christian Bible Fellowship. I was impressed by his love for the ministry that God called him to. When he accepted the invitation to be pastor of our church, he encouraged me to be part of his staff. He mentored me, and from him I learned that serving God is not about ability but availability to God's plan and purpose in one's life. Dr. Oscar's memoir would be a great reading for new pastors on what to expect as they serve the Lord.

Rev. Jemuel Mendoza
Chairman
Philippine Rural Ministries, Inc.

I have known Dr. Oscar Baldemor since we first met in the Philippines 50 years ago. He is a prince among men. Gifted, gracious, and godly, his quiet and thoughtful disposition demonstrates that he has been blessed with unusual discernment and perception. His wise counsel has been a blessing to me personally and it was a rare privilege for me to serve alongside him for several years in the ministries of the Conservative Baptist Association of Southern California. This book is a wonderful account of the marvelous grace of God demonstrated in a life totally surrendered to the Lordship of Jesus Christ. I shall be forever grateful to God for the privilege of knowing him as a beloved brother in Christ and fellow servant in ministry.

Dr. John Redman
Pastor
Grace Bible Church of North Georgia

Introduction

This memoir is a testimony to God's faithfulness. The Lord led our family to know Him and used us to start a church from our home. He gave me the privilege of opening and leading the ministry on different campuses. My experience as a student worker became an asset as I directed the association of churches, followed by church planting and pastoring in the U.S., with exciting twists and turns in between.

This book is about my personal journey. God has amazed and surprised me at every turn. I trust that this will encourage, inspire, and challenge the readers, especially those who are currently in the ministry or are contemplating serving the Lord.

As for my family, I hope that they will be able to appreciate not only what they are now, but also know where they came from. In all of this, God has been there, sustaining us amid life's diverse experiences. I thank the Lord for everything that He has done.

> *"Do you not know?*
> *Have you not heard?*
> *The Lord is the everlasting God,*
> *the Creator of the ends of the earth.*
> *He will not grow tired or weary,*

and his understanding no one can fathom.
He gives strength to the weary
    and increases the power of the weak.
Even youths grow tired and weary,
    and young men stumble and fall;
but those who hope in the Lord
    will renew their strength.
They will soar on wings like eagles;
    they will run and not grow weary,
    they will walk and not faint."

Isaiah 40:28-31

EARLY YEARS

Born in Paete, Laguna, where I spent my formative years, I got both my primary and secondary education in that small town. A former neighbor and classmate in primary school described our town so eloquently:

> "Paete lies at the foot of the green Sierra Madre mountains looking northwest halfway across the water towards Mabitac hill peninsula and on to what seems to be infinity itself. One does not see Manila from here. The silvery water is not the China Sea, but simply Laguna de Bay (Lake of Ba-i), the largest lake in southeast Asia.
>
> Paete is home to the lanzones fruit, the "ukit" (woodcarving), the "bakya" (Philippine wooden shoes), the gaily painted papier-mache *"taka"*, yo-yo, and other toys...and the magical stories, songs, and poems that the people themselves weave in their various celebrations and day-to-day living." (Marie Cagahastian Castillo-Pruden, Paete.org)

Parents

My parents were Estanislao Salceda Baldemor and Dionisia Asido Cainto. My father, whom we called *"Ama"* (Tagalog for father), was a full-time farmer, who

 worked the rice fields from December to May when Laguna de Bay was on low tide and tended the small farm planted with lanzones, coconut, and other fruit-bearing trees up in the Sierra Madre mountains from June to November.

My mother, a housewife, occasionally sold "gaily painted papier-mache" in nearby towns during fiestas to augment the family income. We called her *"Ina"* (Tagalog for mother), who bore and lovingly cared for seven children.

Birth

On March 11, 1943, soldiers of the Japanese Imperial Army arrived in town. They rounded up the residents and told them to gather at the town plaza. Everyone—men, women, and children—with no exception, were required to leave their houses and line up to be identified by *"makapili"* (hooded men) if any of them were spying for the allied forces.

A pregnant woman faced one of the soldiers and pointed to her bulging middle, and somehow was able to communicate that she was about to give birth at any moment. For whatever reason, the soldier made an exception and allowed the woman to stay in her house. Everyone else had to go, including the midwife who was there to assist her in childbirth. While lined up at the plaza, the midwife was able to sneak out from the crowd, unnoticed by the soldiers.

She quickly walked to the pregnant woman's house. By the time she arrived, a baby boy was already out of his mother's womb without any help. He came to this world on his own. I was that baby boy. For reasons unknown to no one, I was spared at birth.

Soon after I was born, our family along with other families, was forced to move out of town since the news spread that towns were being burned down by the retreating forces of the Japanese Imperial Army. Since the town of Paete was sandwiched by the lake on one side and the mountains on the other, the only place to go was up. We retreated to our hut where lights were covered at night so as not to give away our location.

As I was growing up, I often wondered: Why did the Japanese soldier make an exception and allow my mother to remain in the house? What would have happened if my mother was forced to walk to the plaza? Would the baby have survived the ordeal? Obviously, the answer is, God's hand was in all of this. His reason for allowing me to be born would begin to unfold. He had spared me for a purpose.

Religious Family

I grew up in a very religious family, a tradition handed down to us by our paternal grandparents.

Our father's family, consisting of seven brothers and sisters, owned two life-size images—of baby Jesus in a manger and a resurrected Jesus, respectively. These images were kept in my grandparents' house. They were brought to the church every Christmas season and Easter Sunday. My grandparents set aside the income from a parcel of land planted with lanzones and coconut trees to cover the expenses of the two images. They purchased new wardrobes annually for the images so they would look good every time they were displayed before the public. They also applied special perfume on the baby Jesus in a manger so it would smell good when the faithful kissed its feet before leaving the church. People who owned images took care of them in the same way.

When the owners brought back the images from the church, they would prepare a lavish meal in celebration of their "coming home." Everyone in the town was welcome to celebrate. No one was refused.

My family had other involvements in religious practices. On Holy Thursday, my father served as one of the twelve apostles when the priest re-enacted the washing of the feet at the Lord's supper. In our early teens, my brother and I served as altar boys to assist the priest during the mass.

Lastly, it was the tradition to give the images to the eldest son in the family, which happened to be my father. That practice would eventually change when years later, my father politely refused to inherit the images. He had become a Christian, so he requested the brother next in line to keep the images. My father's siblings were not happy with him. Much later, however, they accepted his decision.

FIRST EXPOSURE TO THE GOSPEL

WorldVenture, formerly called Conservative Baptist Foreign Mission Society (CBFMS), sent their first missionaries to the Philippines to the province of Laguna. The reason: According to their research done in the mid-50s, Laguna was one of the least evangelized provinces in Luzon.

After-School Bible Classes

They sent Rev. and Mrs. William Simons who, though residing in San Juan, Metro Manila, went to Laguna regularly on weekends. One of those who joined the couple was a single lady missionary named Beulah Heaton who went to different high schools to teach after-school Bible classes. With Miss Heaton was a Filipina Bible School graduate, Rosalinda Ison.

Bill and Flossie Simons, first missionaries to Laguna

Rosalinda Ison & Beulah Heaton

Among the high schools that they went to was Eastern Laguna Institute where my siblings and I attended. It was the only high school in the town of Paete at that time. My older brother Roger was curious to attend those weekly classes. He was fascinated by the flannel graph figures that the teacher used in telling the Bible stories. During one of those classes, he decided to receive Christ, which opened the way for the missionaries to visit our home.

After several months of hearing the Gospel from them, my eldest sister Dolores, and both our parents, accepted Christ. Joining them was furthest from my mind. I didn't want to associate with the missionaries because I was suspicious of their motive for coming, plus I wasn't confident speaking in English.

Kuya Roger with the after-school Bible class

Sunday Evening Meetings

The after-school Bible class eventually led to Sunday evening meetings held in our home. The missionaries brought with them some Filipino workers: Pastors Jose Galuego, Castro Quimba, Felonito Sacapano, and a layman, Esteban Salcedo. A volunteer worker from

Grace Bible Church in Nagtahan, Manila, also came along. His name was Fred Magbanua, Jr.

As a young boy observing what they were doing in our house, I vividly remember one incident while they were holding their meeting. We had chickens that roamed around freely in the neighborhood. They would come home inside our house to roost when the sun went down.

That Sunday evening, the chickens were making noise because there were people inside and they were blocking the chickens' entrance. The lead hen whom we called "Brownie" flew above us and landed on the bald head of the man who was speaking. Everyone who was listening intently broke out in laughter, including the speaker himself.

The audience knew what they needed to do next. They made a pathway for the chickens to walk through and get settled. Then they encouraged the preacher to go on. They didn't want to embarrass him. Since that time, the Sunday evening meetings did not start until after the chickens had come home. Incidents like this did not deter those pioneer Christian workers from continuing to share the Gospel.

Fast forward to six decades later, the church that started in our home, now called New Testament Baptist Church (NTBC), is one of the most vibrant in the area. It has started six daughter churches, and two of those daughter churches birthed one each. NTBC also founded the Simons Institute of Theology in honor of missionary William Simons who pioneered the work in Laguna.

Salvation and Baptism

As days went by, I began to warm up to the team that came to our home every weekend. One day, I was invited to attend a Christmas program in another town, Santa Maria, and I went. The speaker used pictures that were stuck on the board that aroused my curiosity, the same way they intrigued my brother, Roger, at the after-school class. When an invitation was given, I was among those who accepted Christ, but I told no one. I didn't make a public profession—that was later—but I counted that night as my spiritual birthday. December 23, 1956, was the beginning of my Christian journey.

Much later, I learned that my brother who was then studying at Far Eastern Bible Institute and Seminary (FEBIAS) requested a group at the school to pray for the family, specifically for my salvation. Their prayer was answered.

In August of the following year, I was baptized by missionary William Simons in the murky river amidst water lilies in a neighboring town of Lumban. Since then, I became active in the youth group of our newly formed church. I remember teaching children at the two-week Daily Vacation Bible School one summer. I also joined the Laguna Bible Institute held one night a week at the Simons' home in Pagsanjan. My classmates were elders from the newly formed churches in Laguna.

Summer Camp

In 1958, when I was a sophomore in high school, I attended my first summer camp held at the Nazarene

Bible College in Trinidad Valley near Baguio City. It was my first trip outside of my home province. It was also my first train ride. Young people from different towns in Laguna, Mindoro, Batangas, and Pampanga attended that camp. We took the train in the Tutuban station from Manila to Damortis, La Union, then a bus to Trinidad Valley. That was the first time I was exposed to people from different provinces.

During that week at camp, I heard both Filipino pastors and western missionaries speak from the Bible. wA men's quartet sang at the meetings. We sat in small groups and had Bible study and devotions led by counselors. My counselor was Brother Eleazer Alfonso of San Juan Gospel Chapel. God used that summer camp to help me grow in my spiritual life.

Me as a teenager

MY MOTHER'S ROLE

After I graduated from high school, my mother became concerned about my future. She did not want me to stay in our town where I would end up helping my father tend the farm. She didn't like it because she knew once I got deep into farming, it would be difficult for me to change course. She said, "I don't want you to merely tend the farm like your father. I believe that God has a different purpose for your life."

Different Options

Farmers in our town do not have large areas of land to till. Hence, farmers can hardly support a family. Laguna de Bay's water inundate rice farms half of the year, preventing the farmers from planting other crops when the water is high. Income from farming is limited and needs to be augmented by earning from other crops planted up in the mountains such as coconuts and lanzones. Between harvesting crops from the highland and rice from the lowland are several months of no income.

I wanted to pursue either dentistry, a career in law, or join the U.S. Navy. Several of my high school classmates joined the U.S. Navy. I ended up going to Bible School instead. How did that happen?

My eldest sister was finishing her degree in Education at the Philippine Normal College. My older brother was already in his second year at FEBIAS College of Bible, training for the ministry. He showed much promise as seen by missionaries, pastors, and of course, my parents, especially my mother. In short, he was highly regarded both in school and out.

My mother then talked to me saying, "If you agree to study for a year in Bible school where your brother is currently studying, then you can take any course of your choice." The condition was attending Bible school for a year. I was not too attracted to the offer my mother proposed.

Joining the U.S. Navy became a more attractive alternative. I began inquiring from several sources about joining the Navy. My interest was piqued when I learned about the opportunity to travel around the world while working and earning in U.S. dollars. Without telling anyone, I was imagining this was a good way out of town.

At that point, Sunday evening meetings were held at our home. American missionaries together with Filipino pastors and Bible school students were conducting the worship services. I learned later that one of the missionaries was a former U.S. Navy Chaplain who was assigned at Subic Bay during World War II. His name was William W. Simons. When I mustered enough courage to talk to him about my dream of joining the Navy, I learned that during that time people of color in the Navy had little or no opportunity to move up in rank. They were relegated to washing dishes, cleaning toilets, and other menial jobs. Few, if ever, rose to the rank of officer.

Bible School

Now, my mother's offer was my only option. I had hurdles to overcome, though.

First, I was not prepared emotionally, mentally, and financially to go through this route to fulfill my dream. Secondly, I was not in any way interested in studying at a Bible school even for just a year. Thirdly, I could not see how my parents could possibly support my schooling since the two older siblings were studying full-time in college, though one had a full scholarship.

My mother, however, insisted that I leave town at the soonest possible time before the rice planting season. She told me to pack my belongings but to leave when my father was not home. My father did not suspect something was being planned, orchestrated by my mother. He did not know I was leaving town, which meant he would not have any help on the farm from his second son.

I did not witness how my father reacted when he learned I left home. I found out later that my father did not say a word. I think that's how he trusted my mother's decision. The day my mother sent me away to Bible school, to which I grudgingly agreed, forever altered the trajectory of my life.

Little did I know that my older brother, Roger, asked his prayer group at FEBIAS to pray that I follow him in serving the Lord. That might have influenced my decision to agree with my mother's plan. I was also unaware that he talked to the missionaries to help with my financial support since our parents would not be able to underwrite my studies. The mission group approved his request with a twist. Half of their support was an outright grant, but the other half was a work scholarship, meaning I'd have to work.

A GIRL WITH LONG HAIR

In the mid-50s, mission agencies in Southern and Central Luzon decided to hold annual joint youth camps since there were not enough campers within one mission group. Overseas Missionary Fellowship (OMF), Far Eastern Gospel Crusade (FEGC), and Conservative Baptist Mission (CBM) co-sponsored these youth camps.

Young people, mostly high school students from the provinces of Laguna, Batangas, Oriental Mindoro, and Pampanga were invited to the camp held at the campus of Nazarene Bible College in Trinidad Valley, outside of the city of Baguio. We hardly knew each other since we came from different provinces and churches.

First Impression

At the camp, I saw a young girl with long hair who caught my curiosity and attention. In my mind she stood out among the other girls. She appeared friendly, articulate, bubbly, and impressed me as an intelligent person. She was different and I was drawn to her, even though we had not really met.

As soon as I laid my eyes on her, I thought to myself that one day she would become my wife. We had not formally met, but that's how strong of an impression she had on me. I learned from the other campers that her name was "Lina." I did not, however, have the courage to introduce myself to her. Come to think of it, I did not know how to introduce myself to anyone, period. I did not mix well with the other campers. I was shy, reserved, and unsure of myself. I felt that I had nothing substantial or important to say and if I did, I did not know how to properly express myself.

The week-long youth camp ended without us meeting each other. She was just another camper, a new acquaintance, but deep within me I thought of her as someday becoming my wife. I kept that thought to myself and never shared it with anyone.

After a long train ride from Damortis, La Union, to Manila, the campers went to different bus stations that would take them to their respective provinces and towns. We took the same bus since she came from the same province as I did. When she got off the bus, I handed her a lei made of everlasting flowers that grew in Baguio. She took it. I do not remember if she even looked at it or said "thank you." What I knew was that I gave her a lei hoping she'd remember me. It cost me money I did not have much of. That was the extent of our first encounter. I just hoped that someday our paths would cross again.

Getting Reacquainted

I was pleasantly surprised when I learned that the girl I met at the youth camp in Baguio a few years back had enrolled at FEBIAS, the same institution where I was studying. We were still mere acquaintances but the feeling I had at the youth camp came back. I now had the opportunity to observe her closely while at school. In doing so, I continued to want to know her more. I was not aware she was sharing her feelings towards me with a dorm mate who was from my hometown. Our mutual friend was giving hints to me about her feelings towards me. At this point, we had become friends. It was becoming obvious that we had feelings toward each other. On March 23, 1963, I asked her if she would be willing to go steady. Without hesitation, she said "yes." Upon hearing her response, I said, "Let's pray." I suggested committing this new level of relationship to the Lord in prayer before she could change her mind.

From that day on the two of us became an "item," a relationship that was encouraged by the faculty and staff at FEBIAS.

Our dates were supervised, usually at the apartment of Mrs. Mary Judson, the dean of women. Holding hands was not allowed even when we walked side-by-side to and from the women's dorm, the library, the classroom, and the dining hall. The strict rules caused us to be creative, mostly with the written word as we exchanged notes and letters almost daily. I think I wrote her over 30 letters in a span of two years, while she sent me about 200, using not only stationery but also barks of trees, paper napkins, and other things she could write on.

When we were dating

Saying "I Do"

On July 4, 1967, we exchanged vows at her home church in Santa Cruz, Laguna. Our wedding was officiated by missionary William Simons, the man who first brought the Gospel to my family and baptized me. He was assisted by Rev. Ernie Montealegre, Lynn's pastor. My Kuya Roger was my best man, while a close missionary friend, Marilyn Sonmor, served as her matron of honor. She and her husband Steve also sang at the ceremony. Frank Obien, who recruited me to join CCC staff played the organ while his wife, Rosie, sang a special song. That amazing day, the girl with long hair named Lina Bautista, whom I first saw back at the youth camp a decade before, became my wife—Mrs. Lina B. Baldemor!

TRAINING YEARS

I went to FEBIAS, not knowing much about the Bible except what I learned at the Laguna Bible Institute. Without much background, I did not know what to expect.

School Rules

The dormitories were Quonset huts made of World War II surplus materials. Since the school was started by American GIs, they were able to obtain such from the military bases. The dorm was a big hall lined with bunk beds, military style.

We followed strict rules and schedules: times to wake up, devotions, meals, attend classes, lights out, and so forth. There was a daily bed inspection. Everything had to be neat and organized. I also learned to wash and iron my clothes. I got used to following rules though it was difficult at first.

I gradually learned to study, something that I never did in high school. I learned how to read my Bible. I wasn't consistent in doing my devotions before that.

We had a demerit system. The number of demerits was based on infractions. Minor ones included untidy beds, shoes or slippers not arranged properly, being late for classes, etcetera. Other offenses included not observing personal devotion at the designated time, skipping classes, missing chapel, and making noise or talking after lights out at 11:00 pm. Once a student reached a certain number of demerits, they received disciplinary action. I was one of those always on the brink of reaching the limit of demerits; close, but not quite. I followed the rules, though grudgingly at times. Later when I finished school, I realized that obeying the rules helped form my character.

At FEBIAS, I was fascinated by the way people communicated with one another, because that was my weakest point. I compared myself with my classmates who grew up in the city and spoke English fluently.

It was tough studying and working at the same time. I only had a partial scholarship, so I had to work for the remainder of my tuition. I worked as a dishwasher, a librarian, and a yardman at different times. I also served as a night security guard, working a two-hour shift each time.

Turning Point

I learned early on how to preach mostly in Tagalog, my native tongue. Even though I was getting better at it, I was not sure if preaching was my calling. I did not know what I should do, whether to pursue the ministry. Then in September 1964, one year before I graduated, the FEBIAS president, Dr. Russell Honeywell, talked to me one early morning at the end of my shift.

"Young man," he said, "what are you thinking of doing when you leave this place?"

I don't remember what else we talked about, but that morning, I decided to serve the Lord full-time. Dr. Honeywell then prayed for me. I became more serious in my studies and in my life. Little did I know that I was being observed by the faculty and staff. They saw changes in me.

In my senior year, I began to enjoy studying and serving the Lord. One opportunity was leading the singing at "Youth Time," a weekly evangelistic gathering at UP PGH, a public hospital, sponsored by Christ for Greater Manila (CGM).

Then during the Christmas break in 1964, I had the privilege of being part of a team composed of graduating FEBIAS students that surveyed the Bondoc peninsula in the province of Quezon. It was led by FEGC (now SEND International) missionaries Cliff Bedell and Ty Kersey. We started in the town of Gumaca, all the way to Catanauan, traveling on rough, muddy roads. We conducted evangelistic meetings in the evenings.

Senior class, 1965

ONE SUMMER

When I was 19 years old, I was assigned to work as a student pastor in Bago Bantay, Quezon City, during a summer break from FEBIAS. Capitol City Baptist Church (CCBC) just opened a work in the area which at that time was a relocation site for informal settlers (formerly called squatters). In addition to families, gangs lived there, and rival groups often engaged in fights and brawls. In the 1960s, Bago Bantay was not the safest place to be.

Bago Bantay Experience

Three things stand out in my mind from that summer of 1962.

First, the church meetings were held at the *silong* or ground floor of the house of Mr. and Mrs. Alonzo (not their real name), a couple who were new Christians. While meetings or Bible studies were going on, one could hear the rival gangs fighting outside.

We often witnessed fist fights. We also saw darts flying around as the gang members used them to protect their turf. Both adult men and young men engaged in drinking after dark, their favorite pastime. During that time, very few people owned a television set.

Second, I stayed in one of the rooms of the Alonzos' house and I could hear them quarreling almost daily. The wife was a retired boxer while the husband was a jiu jitsu black belter. The couple often asked me to mediate between them, and most of the time, I was able to calm them down. One morning, the man knocked on my door to borrow my sunglasses. The reason: His wife punched him, and he didn't want to go to work with a visible blackeye!

Third, the most significant time was when we held an open-air evangelistic meeting. The speaker was a 6' 4" tall American, Don Benson, who was a varsity wrestler in college. He was trying to practice his Tagalog. A guy who just came from work, slightly drunk but still able to walk, heard Don and became curious about a foreigner speaking Tagalog. He stopped to listen. Although a bit drunk, he listened intently to the message and decided to receive Christ that night. His name: Antonio Ordinaria.

Tony

It was my privilege to follow up with Tony and help him grow in his new-found relationship with Jesus Christ.

Tony sharing Christ at a medical mission

One day he told me that he wanted to go to a Bible school, so I encouraged him to enroll at FEBIAS. He studied there for three years but dropped out for financial reasons.

Then he found a job as an electrical inspector at the Quezon City Fire Department.

Even then, he continued to serve the Lord. While working at the Fire Department, he helped start a church at Krus na Ligas in Quezon City, near UP, together with folks from CCBC, including Percy and Priscilla Damazo, Adela Flores, and Col. Sinforiano Rosario.

Tony and I developed a very close friendship. I served as best man at his wedding. He became ninong (godfather) to our eldest daughter.

Years later, he and his wife, Vennie Javelosa, moved to Lagro Subdivision to a house awarded to them by the government. As a bi-vocational pastor, Tony started a church in Lagro which produced several young people who went into the ministry, just like the church in Krus na Ligas.

All this time, Tony and I remained close friends, even after they went to the U.S. his wife was employed as a teacher on a working visa with Tony as her dependent. While in Texas, Tony started a church in McAllen where they resided. I had the opportunity to visit them on several occasions, even speaking at one of their summer camps.

Saying Goodbye

Tony and Vennie joined our medical mission in Laoag City, Philippines, in 2007. The following year, Tony was diagnosed with cancer. They opted to travel to the Philippines for treatment. They wanted to join the medical mission again, but Tony was too weak and was admitted to the hospital instead.

When I visited him at the National Kidney and Transplant Institute in Quezon City, he requested his guests and even his wife to leave the room so the two of us could be alone.

Then he said, "Oscar, I don't think I'll make it this time. Thank you for all that you did for me. I enjoyed our time together. I will see you in heaven." With tears, we prayed together. I asked the Lord to prolong my friend's life, but God had another plan.

Tony went to heaven before his daughter could get married. The following year, Lynn and I flew to Dallas, Texas, where I had the privilege of walking his daughter down the aisle in Tony's place.

Looking back at that summer in Bago Bantay, I almost quit the ministry because of the discouraging environment and difficult people to work with. BUT, because of Tony, the Lord picked me up and encouraged me to move on.

INTERNSHIP YEAR

After graduation in May 1965, Capitol City Baptist Church (CCBC) invited me to be an intern under missionary Art Beals and Pastor Fred Magbanua. I welcomed that opportunity because having grown up in the province, I really wanted to be exposed to working in an urban setting. My internship lasted for a year and a half.

Assignments

As a single guy, I stayed at the church basement together with the custodian. My main responsibilities as an intern were conducting home Bible studies on weeknights, leading the youth group, and preaching at the Junior Church worship. I remember teaching the kids about cultural minorities (tribes people) and how they needed to hear the Gospel. Every night, I went to a different home to teach Bible classes using materials coming from Christ for Greater Manila's (CGM) Project Philip. I brought several Good News Bibles with me so that class members could use the same translation.

As part of my internship program, I read and critiqued one book a month. I met with the two pastors on a regular basis to discuss the book and to report on the progress of my ministry.

Plaza Miranda

One thing that I enjoyed doing during my internship was going to Plaza Miranda in front of the Quiapo Church on my nights off to watch one man after another talk about various topics, mostly religious perspectives. I was intrigued hearing their arguments as they debated. When one could not answer or ran out of things to say, he simply left the group and let others take a turn. Occasionally, I joined in the debates.

When CGM conducted an open-air evangelistic campaign at Plaza Miranda, they invited me to be one of the speakers. They had me use a flip chart with illustrations from the "Four Spiritual Laws." I didn't even know about that booklet. I simply explained the drawings the best I knew how. I think they liked how I did it, so CGM director Will Bruce asked me to be on their staff, but I politely turned him down because I did not have peace accepting the offer.

A Surprise Visit

One day in November, a man named Frank Obien came to see me at the CCBC basement.

"Are you Oscar Baldemor?"

"Yes."

"My name is Frank Obien. I'm with Campus Crusade for Christ." And he went on to tell me about a new organization in town which he represented. Then he said, "Someone heard you speak at Plaza Miranda using a handwritten flip chart with a message like the Four Spiritual Laws. We are looking for people to work with us. I would like to invite you to be on the staff of

Crusade. Let me give you an application form. You may fill it out and I will come back in a few days to pick it up."

I thought to myself, "I'm applying?" But I did fill out the application, Obien picked it up as he promised, and informed me later that I was accepted on staff. My training would begin on the first working day of January 1967.

CAMPUS CRUSADE FOR CHRIST
Part 1

My training as staff began in January 1967. At that time, the two top leaders of Philippine Campus Crusade for Christ (now known as Cru), Guillermo Bergado and Frank Obien lived at 21-B and 21-F Timog Avenue in Quezon City. Their homes also served as the office.

Training

Frank handed me the staff manual and instructed me to read a chapter a day, then I took an exam after each chapter. The manual was basically what Crusade was all about, how it began, its philosophy of ministry, etc. I was introduced to the name Bill Bright, president and founder of the organization.

The reading portion of my training was in the morning, where I became familiar with the strategy of evangelizing students by going to the campuses using a small yellow booklet called, Four Spiritual Laws. I was asked to memorize it and practice using it.

In the afternoon, the practicum was going to the UP Diliman campus and sharing Christ using the Four Spiritual Laws booklet.

University of the Philippines

The first day was quite interesting. I did not know how to approach people and what to say to introduce the Four Spiritual Laws. There I was at the AS (Arts and Sciences) building lobby looking for a "prospect" who didn't look busy. Finally, I found someone who seemed to be a little lost. I took off my watch, put it in my pocket, and asked the guy, "Excuse me, what time is it?" He checked his watch and gave me the time.

Then I said, "If you have time, there's something I'd like to share with you." He agreed. We went outside, sat under a tree, and I read to him the Four Spiritual Laws booklet. When I reached the end, I asked if he would like to accept Christ and he said yes. I led him in a prayer of acceptance. His name was Hexel Hernando, a freshman.

That was my first day on campus. I was not only surprised but also happy that the guy prayed to receive Christ. Years later when *Papuri!* (Praise) songs (original Filipino Christian music) became popular, Hexel wrote and composed *Mahal Ka ng Diyos* (God Loves You), which became a favorite in many churches up to this day.

The following day, I went to the same place where I met another young man. I asked him if he had heard of the Four Spiritual Laws, and he said no. I shared the booklet with him and to my surprise he bowed his head and prayed with me to ask Christ into his heart. His name was Gil Diokno. At the time of this writing, Gil is pastoring a church in West Virginia, U.S.A.

I continued to share Christ daily at UP but there were times when Frank would ask me to go with him to the University of Manila (UM). He was then forming a university choir which later became known as the CCC choir. I was able to share with UM students also, including a Muslim guy, who at first indicated his interest in Jesus. He stopped coming because he could not accept the teaching that Jesus resurrected from the dead.

Aside from one-on-one sharing, we went into student dormitories and showed a film featuring André Kole, a Christian illusionist. He captured the audience with his illusion, then at the end he gave an invitation to consider the claims of Christ.

Part of our immersion in the UP community was applying to be recognized as a campus organization. We found a faculty adviser, Professor Alice Amen of the Engineering Department, and submitted our Constitution and By-laws along with a list of student officers. We were readily approved and allowed to put up a UP CCC bulletin board at the AS lobby adjacent to the Business Administration building which became a hang-out of our student contacts. As a legitimate organization, we were not only able to come in every day without being questioned by security, but we were also invited to join campus events such as the hayride, tree-planting on Arbor Day, etc.

"College Life" was another activity that we did to reach students. We held this gathering on the second floor of Vinson Hall. We invited speakers. Some of those who spoke were Ambassador Tiburcio Baja, Dr. Dale

Brunner, and Pastor Richard Wurmbrand who wrote *Tortured for Christ*.

When College Life meetings became a weekly gathering, we moved to larger venues to accommodate more students. The program also evolved from a lecture type forum with a question-and-answer time to an informal fellowship that included lively group singing, testimonies of new Christians, and occasional skits. It always ended with a "clincher" (Gospel presentation], and a pray-with-me invitation. We served punch and cookies while the students mingled and chatted. Some sat together in groups of two or more, praying and discussing the message they just heard.

College Life also encouraged musically inclined students to form singing groups that performed at the meetings. The first group was called "UPCCC Certain Sounds," composed of Gil Diokno, Nick Chan, Ed Nibut, Francie Castañeda, Cecile Mandac, Sonia Carreon, and Bethel Diokno.

Certain Sounds, circa 1969. From left: Francie Castañeda, Cecile Mandac, Gil Diokno, Nick Chan, Ed Nibut, Bethel Diokno, and Sonia Carreon.

Later, four guys formed the "Big Brat Band": Hexel Hernando, Philip Tarroja, Nelson Sarcos, and Gil Diokno. The two singing groups combined and added a few more members to form "God's Forever Family."

Some of the staff who worked at UP in the early days. Front row: Olive Sarte, Thelly Contado, Lynn Baldemor, Precy Manongdo. Back row: Romy Santos, Emer Nicer, Oscar Baldemor.

In the summer, we sponsored camps and training retreats where many students were challenged to serve the Lord by joining staff.

We saw even more growth in the UP work with the coming of Kent Hutcheson whose specialty was training.

University of the East

As the ministry at UP progressed, I saw that we were putting a lot of effort into that campus, but no one was going to other schools. I asked permission to go to the University Belt and was readily approved. I took with me a guy named Tony Ruiz. A friend of Frank Obien, Tony was not quite finished with his Engineering course so he enrolled at University of the East (UE) in order that he could help me there.

I invited about 25 UP students to open the work at UE by doing a one-day witnessing "blitzkrieg." They scattered around the UE campus talking to students using the Four Spiritual Laws booklet. It was very conspicuous that almost everywhere people turned, there was someone sharing, holding a little yellow booklet. This did not escape the attention of security guards.

One of the guards reported it to the chief of security, who asked for the leader of the group. It did not take long to find me. Two guards escorted me to the security office. The chief of security asked what I was doing on campus, what group I was with, and why we were there.

Of course, as a trained CCC staff member, I said we were there to share a revolution of love, and proceeded to ask, "Sir, have you heard of the Four Spiritual Laws?" When he said "No," I went on to share with him. In the middle of my presentation, he said, "This is not my area of expertise. Let me send you to the dean of student affairs who can better deal with this kind of situation." He then motioned to the two security guards standing by to escort me to the office of the dean.

At the office of the dean of student affairs, they asked the same questions that the chief of security asked. I gave the same answers. The dean listened while I shared with him the Four Spiritual Laws. Before I could finish the fourth law, he said, "This is the kind of organization that we need on campus, but before we can recognize you officially, you have to be an approved student organization with the proper credentials." He then instructed me to submit a Constitution and By-laws with a list of officers who were bona fide UE students, along with the name of a faculty adviser.

Excited, I hurriedly conferred with the students from UP and UE and we immediately worked on what was required. Having gone through the process at UP, we used the same Constitution and By-laws, changed the name of the school, names of the officers, and faculty adviser.

Tony Ruiz, who was now a UE student, was appointed president, while another man, Gideon Umandap, was listed as one of the officers. A faculty member who was a leader at Faith Bible Church in Quezon City, Mrs. Paz Loyola, was asked to be the adviser and she readily agreed. In three days, we were officially recognized as a legitimate student organization!

It did not take long for us to recruit more students. After about one semester, UECCC became known, not because of its size, but because of its visibility. Student leaders boldly shared with their fellow students. The administration noticed this and asked our group to serve as Commission on Election (Comelec) during that year's student council election. We tried our best despite lack of experience and lack of personnel.

When Martial Law was declared in the country in September 1972, non-students could no longer get into the campuses without proper identification. We were forced to change our strategy. We could not hold large meetings because gatherings were suspected of being subversive. Even small group meetings on campus were affected. We had to meet in restaurants, but they were not quiet and not conducive to conversation. Time to meet was also limited. Work continued to grow but it was slowed down by Martial Law restrictions.

Far Eastern University

After a year, I turned my attention to a nearby school—Far Eastern University (FEU). The UE work had upcoming leaders who could handle the ministry there.

When I opened the FEU ministry, I had to obtain a day pass from the security guards at the gate every time I went on campus. I told them I was visiting someone. After a while, my face became familiar to them and sometimes they would not let me in. One day, instead of giving me a temporary pass, they sent me to the security office. The chief was Major Moran, who was a little more open to hearing about Christ, but just like the UE security chief, he did not know what to do with me. He then instructed his men to bring me to the executive secretary to the president of the university, Mrs. Sarah Joaquin. I learned later that she was the one who ran the daily affairs of the school.

After hearing what I had to say, she told me to do the same thing that UE required: Constitution and By-laws, list of officers, though she didn't ask for a faculty adviser. Within a few days, she issued 10 official permanent visitor I.D.s for me and my team, signed by her and recognized by all the security officers.

RBJ Building

The problem of meeting in groups inside FEU campus was still a challenge, just like at UE. I didn't realize that not far from that school, the owner of the RBJ Building, Mr. Ricardo B. Jumawan, was building a second floor. RBJ, as his friends called him, was a member and chairman of the board of CCBC, my home church. He had been hearing about our work with students. One day he asked if I needed a meeting place. When I said yes, he gave me this challenge: "I will not put a partition on the second floor. It will just be a big hall. Do you think you could fill it with people in six months?"

For whatever reason, I agreed. The second floor of the RBJ building became the center of activities in the University Belt. We held large group gatherings called "college life" and small group meetings called "discovery group." Students also hung out there.

With RBJ

By this time the ministry had spread to several schools: Mapua Institute, Philippine School of Business Administration, National University, Pamantasan ng Lungsod ng Maynila, University of Santo Tomas, Centro Escolar University, Manila Central University, to name a few.

In six months' time, the second floor of the RBJ Building was filled with people every Friday night for College Life. Around 300 people sat on the floor singing together, watching skits, listening to testimonies of new Christians, and hearing a clear Gospel presentation. I had the privilege of speaking each time, challenging the audience to consider the claims of Christ.

Other Student Leaders

God raised several leaders at the University Belt. One of them was Carlos Ani whom we met at one of 18 classroom presentations at FEU. He accepted Christ at a Leadership Training Institute at Teacher's Camp in Baguio with Mar Santos, a UP student leader. Today, Carlos serves as an elder of Evangelical Baptist Church near UP Los Baños.

The campus ministry spread out to different provinces and cities. As National Campus Director, part of my responsibilities was to visit staff members in other areas. In Cebu, Romy and Olive Santos were the ministry leaders. After holding a week of classroom evangelism at Southwestern University, we took a break and went to a nearby beach. There, I was introduced to a young graduate from Leyte, named Teody Pajaron. He shared with me his desire to be in the ministry. I challenged him to join the staff, which he did. He became part of my team at FEU.

Years later, after serving as National Director of Cru Philippines, Teody went to Western Seminary in Portland, Oregon, where he obtained his Doctor of Missiology degree. When he and his wife Evelyn returned to the Philippines, they founded FamilyLife, a ministry of Cru. As of this writing, the Pajarons are celebrating their 49th anniversary as staff.

CAMPUS CRUSADE FOR CHRIST
Part 2

When Martial Law was declared in 1972, the military went around the different university and college campuses in Metro Manila and "invited" students who were perceived as being against the government. Hundreds of students, along with some peasants and government officials, were placed in detention cells in different parts of the country.

Camp Vicente Lim

At one point, CCC was invited to talk to the detainees by then Major Honesto Isleta of the Office of Civil Relations (OCR). Some of our student leaders knew him personally. Campus Crusade was assigned to Camp Vicente Lim in Canlubang, Laguna. I took with me some student leaders from the University Belt who were actively involved in the ministry.

When we arrived at Camp Vicente Lim, they ushered us to the office of the camp commander, Gen. Navarro. He gave us instructions on what we were to do. He also said that the people whom he had chosen to attend our meetings were mostly students. He explained to us why we were there, "We want you to tell them of another kind of revolution, a revolution of the heart." Apparently, he had read the book that we had been passing around, *Revolution Now* by Bill Bright.

At the end of the day, we reported back to Gen. Navarro. He thanked us for our visit. It was a unique experience for all of us.

Jesus March

At that time, street demonstrations were a common scene, mostly sponsored and organized by students. Classes were often disrupted. Sometimes people could not get through in the streets because of demonstrations, especially at Claro M. Recto and Mendiola streets around the University Belt.

CCC decided to do a "Jesus March," proclaiming that there was an excellent alternative to what the demonstrators were shouting.

For several days, we prepared for the Jesus March rally and made our own placards. We chose the Welcome Rotonda on Quezon Blvd. as our starting point. From there we marched all the way to Espana, Morayta, and on to Quiapo. Ending up at Plaza Miranda, the participants climbed on to the stage that was used by politicians from different political parties for their campaign. As I stood on the stage to speak, I saw the hole created by the grenade that was thrown during a political rally a few weeks before.

Our crowd was not as big as the other rallies, but we were big enough to be noticed by the media and the military. Students from colleges and universities all over Metro Manila and representatives from different

ONE WAY, JESUS WAY! ONE WAY, JESUS WAY!

religious groups joined us. We passed out flyers while marching, chanting, "One Way, Jesus Way," with our right hand raised, index finger pointing upwards.
In that rally, several students shared testimonies of salvation. I spoke and shared the message of Christ, the Way, the Truth, and the Life.

One of the results of the Jesus March, which we did twice, was our students got bolder, able to express the change that happened in their lives. They became more inspired and confident in witnessing.

Leadership Training Institute

The Leadership Training Institute, or LTI for short, was held twice a year, but the summer one had a bigger attendance and usually lasted for one week.

LTI was a week of training on how to witness, emphasizing on witnessing as a way of life, using the Four Spiritual Laws booklet. We also included workshops on basic skills like how to prepare a personal testimony. One important part of LTI was going out in the community two-by-two and talking to people about Christ. Then we would come back together and have a time of sharing, noting how many people were shared with and how many prayed to receive Christ. The evening plenary sessions featured messages and challenges from the Word. The first two or three LTIs were held at the UP Los Baños (UPLB) campus. We used the university dormitories for accommodation and the auditorium for our big meetings. Every year, more and more people attended LTI. We usually had more people from the University Belt. Another venue aside from UPLB was a resort at Nalinac in San Fernando, La Union. When the attendance got even larger, we went to the Teachers' Camp in Baguio City.

It was my job to speak at the last night's plenary session which we dubbed "Special Night." That was the time I challenged the students to be involved in full-time service. In our mind, the meaning of full-time service was joining staff. Dozens of students stood up in response to that invitation while lighting candles and singing "Pass It On." It was always solemn and meaningful.

I think the most significant result of LTI was the decision made by students who joined the staff. To date, I would connect from time to time with some of those who are now in full-time service, who testify that they were challenged to serve God during their week at LTI.

After the Rains

Another ministry that we got involved in was initiated by our more socially conscious students, and that was to extend help to those affected by calamities, especially typhoons. On several occasions, we gathered mostly food stuff like rice and canned goods and distributed them.

The Office of Civil Relations (OCR) of the military took notice of us and provided trucks for our use. This was in Napindan, Taguig, Rizal, and San Pedro, Laguna. In the severely flooded towns, we used *bancas* or canoes and handed sacks of goods to people who were standing on top of roofs (their houses were partly submerged). As a result of these relief efforts, our students became more involved in their respective communities.

Our youngest volunteer, five-year-old Chinky, placing Four Spiritual Laws booklets inside food bags.

Great Commission Training Center

One of my main responsibilities was the training of potential leaders from different Asian countries. Several of them were being prepared to head their ministry in their respective countries. I brought them to the campuses and had them observe how things should be done. My personal trainees were guys from Indonesia, Japan, Pakistan, Sri Lanka, Cambodia, and Singapore.

By the way, while I was writing this section, I received a call asking if I could give a short greeting to congratulate Pastor Taing Vek Huong, my former trainee in CCC from Cambodia. He and his wife Samouen were being honored by their church, New Life Church of Phnom Penh, for their 50 years of service. Pastor Vek was also the voice of Jesus in the *Jesus Film* in Khmer.

My associate pastor and I met with two former Cru trainees, Teody Pajaron (second from the left) and Karel Pattipelohy from Indonesia (far right)

THROUGH THE VALLEY
by Lynn Baldemor

Oscar and I first tasted the joy of parenthood when our baby was born on April 19, 1968, almost a year from the day we were married!

Enter Timothy Carl

That day, Oscar went to UP while I spent time in the home of Guil and Betty Bergado, Campus Crusade staff, working on placards for an upcoming student demonstration. Before too long, I began feeling pains around my middle. Having given birth to four children, Betty was able to tell that my time had come. She immediately phoned for help. I was taken to the Children's Memorial Hospital where Oscar and my obstetrician, Dr. Santiago del Rosario, met up with us.

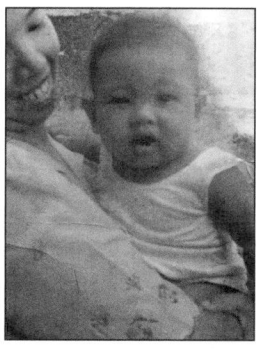

A few hours later, the doctor handed me a beautiful, fair-skinned, almost bald baby boy all wrapped in a light blue blanket. Overwhelmed, I looked at the baby and said softly, "Is he really ours?" We named him "Timothy" from the Bible and "Carl" from the last three letters of Oscar's name and the first letter of mine, so, "Timothy Carl" was his name, but we just called him Carl for short.

Smart Child

A precocious and happy child, Carl started talking before he was two, almost already in complete sentences. One day he lined up half-opened books on the floor, domino-style, then announced proudly, "Look, make book stand." Another time, he acknowledged my feeble attempt at the piano by saying, "Mommy, play 'Jesus Loves Me'."

Our two-year-old enjoyed being with people. We didn't own a television set then, so our neighbors at the apartment complex several doors from us often "borrowed" Carl so he could watch cartoons with them. He told them that he would like to have his own TV.

One day when I picked him up from the neighbors' apartment, Carl kept walking past our door.

"Hey, where are you going?" I asked.

"To the store in front to buy a T.V."

Well, that little *sari-sari* (convenience) store only sold snacks and a few kitchen necessities!

Another time, Carl and I walked to the open market not far from our place. Some people were on the street. As he watched them, he commented that he wanted to have shoes like grown-ups wore (meaning dress shoes). As we walked, we saw a crippled child being pushed in a cart. He had no feet. Grasping a golden teaching moment, I asked, "Carl, what would you prefer, to have shoes but no feet, or just feet but no shoes?" He replied, "Mommy, I want to have feet (pause. . .) and shoes, too!" Hmm.

At age two and a half, our son was already a big brother. I felt that I got pregnant with my daughter too soon, but God had other plans. Carl enjoyed having a little sister, nicknamed "Chinky," whom he alternately played with and bossed around. She was a little over a year old and already quite feisty.

When he got an early Christmas present, a small bike, from his godfather, Carl wanted the baby to ride it with him, but of course she couldn't.

Kids and Ministry

Having two little ones at home limited my involvement with the ministry. I tried my best to help, so when we were asked to temporarily host Asian trainees, I was eager to comply. That meant moving into the Hutcheson home to take care of the trainees.

At that time, Kent and Diane Hutcheson had just moved to the Philippines to start a CCC international training center. Before they could settle, however, they had to fly to the U.S. to be with a very ill parent. So, when we agreed to host the trainees, it meant moving our whole family to the Hutcheson home.

The first three trainees had just arrived in Manila: an Indonesian couple, Karel and Emma Pattipelohy and a young Japanese guy, Yasuhiko Akatsu. Not only did they stay with us, but they also ate their meals with us. I was thankful to have my sister-in-law, Nelia, and a live-in helper, Naomi, around to help with housework and the babies.

Having a helper also freed me to go on campus occasionally with Oscar. We were quite excited one Wednesday as we, UP Campus Crusade staff and students, got ready to host a party for the student council among whom were Miriam Defensor, Franklin Drillon, and Richard Gordon (as of this writing, currently prominent figures in Philippine politics, except for Miriam who passed away a few years ago). We had been working on campus that day, but we went home for a bit to check on the kids.

As I laid down my purse on the counter, Carl asked if I had candy. I said I didn't and walked to the kitchen, but he didn't follow me. Then I heard a loud CRASH! Carl had tried to climb on the detachable counter, and it fell on him!

"I Want to Sleep"

Oscar and I took our son in a taxi to the Orthopedic Hospital, thinking that he might have broken a rib. As our cab sliced through the afternoon Quezon Boulevard traffic, Carl quietly watched cars and buses outside the window. He wasn't even crying. He whispered to my husband, "I want to sleep."

At the hospital, doctors and nurses immediately operated on him. My husband and I prayed and begged God to spare our son's life. Then I shared with Oscar God's Word that He gave me a few days before.

The Saturday before our son's accident, I reluctantly attended a women's meeting at our church. At age 25, I felt I was too young to be part of that group of older women. I went only because the speaker was Mrs. Betty Honeywell, my friend and former teacher at FEBIAS. She told the story of the woman of Shunem, from 2 Kings 4. The woman and her husband often invited Elisha, the man of God, to eat with them and even provided him a room whenever he was in their area. One day the couple's son died of a sunstroke but when the man of God inquired about him, she said, "It shall be well." Elisha proceeded to pray for the boy, and he lived again.

I thanked Mrs. Honeywell for her message and apologized for not visiting with her longer because I had to go and make dinner for our Asian house guests. Mom Honeywell enthused, "Oh, this passage applies to you, because you're being hospitable, like the Shunammite woman!" Little did I know that the rest of the story would speak to me, too.

While we waited outside the Operating Room, I shared with my husband the words, "It shall be well," and we asked God one more time to spare Carl's life. A few hours later, our son went to be with Jesus.

Why, despite our plea? The doctor explained to us the extent of our baby's injury. He had 18 major lacerations and they fixed him, but he died of internal bleeding. If he had survived, he would have been severely disabled—unable to walk, run, much less ride his little bike. Through our tears, we thanked the Lord for two years and seven months with our son, and for making him well—in heaven. That was Wednesday, December 2, 1970.

In the meantime, God comforted me with His Word. I read in Psalm 40:1-3, *"I waited patiently for the Lord; he turned to me and heard my cry. He lifted me out of the slimy pit, out of the mud and mire; he set my feet on a rock and gave me a firm place to stand. He put a new song in my mouth, a hymn of praise to our God. Many will see and fear the Lord and put their trust in him."*

A New Song

When Mom Honeywell came to see us at CCBC where Carl's body lay, I shared with her these words of comfort from Psalm 40. She became thoughtful as she murmured, "Hmmm, a new song." The following day she came back and told me, "Lynn, here's the new song that the Lord has given you." And she showed me a poem that she just wrote entitled, "It Shall be Well." A missionary with Far East Broadcasting Company (FEBC), Norman Reiger, had put the poem into music and had graciously offered to sing it at the funeral!

On Saturday, December 5, family and friends, staff, students, and church members packed the church for Carl's final service. As the congregation sang "When He Cometh (Precious Jewels)," "God is So Good," and Carl's favorite, "Jesus Loves Me," it felt as if my chest would explode. Norm Reiger sang the song that Mom Honeywell wrote which brought incredible comfort to my soul. A few students expressed to us later how Carl's death caused them to seriously consider the claims of Christ that many of us staff had shared with them.

"IT SHALL BE WELL"

The path of life for me
Since Jesus set me free
Throbbed joy and victory!
Now walls of fire I see,
Can it be well?

Chorus:

"It shall be well!" Like sunshine through the rain;
"It shall be well!" Faith sings the sweet refrain;
My Father's in control, no blight shall scar my soul,
"It shall be well with me--all shall be well!

2nd Verse:

Tho' typhoon furies blow,
Tho' rising floods o'erflow,
Tho' trouble's clouds hang low,
Yet in the end, I know
"It shall be well!"

3rd Verse:

Tho' death has snatched away
Life's very brightest ray,
Hope sees a future Day;
My tremb'ling lips can say,
"It shall be well!"

4th Verse:

Tho' earthquakes shake the ground;
Tho' wars of hate abound;
If missiles crash around,
Safety in Christ is found--
All shall be well.

Dedicated to Oscar and Lina Baldemor
on the death of Baby Carl.

(Taken from the story of the Woman of
Shunem, II Kings 4:23)

--Betty Honeywell--

That night, Oscar and I prayed and asked the Lord if He would give us another son. A year later, He did.

"Even though I walk through the valley of the shadow of death, I will fear no evil, for you are with me." Psalm 23:4

Oscar's Thoughts

When we lost Carl, I was distraught, discouraged, confused, angry, and bitter all at the same time. I did not know what to think. I could not process what just happened. So many questions flooded my mind. I asked God,

- "Why did you take away our son, why him and not the unwanted, abandoned children roaming the streets?"

- "Am I not serving you full-time already? What else would you want me to do?"

- "Did I do something that displeased you so much that you must take away our son whom we loved so dearly?"

These were some of the questions that went through my mind. While going through the pain and agony of losing my only son, I was accusing God of being unfair in His dealings with me.

Prior to the tragedy, I entertained the idea of leaving the ministry and getting a better paying job so I could provide a decent life to my growing family. Whether my son's passing away had something to do with my plan, I will never know.

Thankfully, the bitterness that I felt did not last long. While the funeral service was in progress, the Spirit's comfort and peace enveloped me, when the congregation sang, "It Is Well, It Is Well with My Soul."

GOD HAS GIVEN
by Lynn Baldemor

It was twilight. The deepening shadows comforted two heartbroken parents who, hours earlier, had buried their two-and-a-half-year-old son. Desperately clinging to each other, they begged God to please, if it be His will, to give them another son.

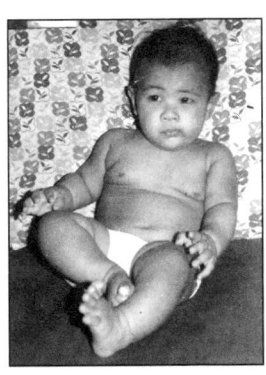

Almost a year later, on September 7, 1971 at the St. Luke's Hospital about an hour away from where they lived, the couple's second son was born. They named him "Jonathan," which from the Hebrew meant "God has given" or "gift from God." The couple was us, and the baby was Jay. His middle name was Carl, from his brother, hence, "Jonathan Carl," but we decided to just call him "Jay." That day, we thanked God for giving him to us and we prayed that he might serve the Lord someday.

As a child, Jay loved to draw, read books, and ride his bike. He often translated special experiences in his young life to sketches and drawings. Once, he tried to illustrate a story that I wrote. He also did simple animation, drew a series of pictures on several pieces of paper to create movement, put them together in a flip book and called it, "Super, Super Fire."

As a young student, he was fascinated by science facts that he learned at school so when he came home, he would make a beeline to our set of encyclopedias and between snacks, read up more on whatever it was that they talked about in class. Riding his bike in the neighborhood was how he made friends. But when he was getting lanky, his hand got caught on his bike's wheel and that's how he lost part of a finger.

Being the only boy, Jay spent many memorable times with his three sisters: joking with them, playing table games, putting on a puppet show, watching television, talking (seriously at times), even fixing their hair for special occasions! They also liked going to church together, although he didn't want to get baptized until his best friend, Bong, could also be baptized.

As a young man, Jay refused to be without a job. He first worked at McDonald's, then at Kinko's, and later at Oaktree. He even sold Cutco Cutlery. He also designed

greeting cards, sold them to a card company, and worked many other odd jobs. Although he dropped out from Long Beach City College, his passion and skill with technology landed him a job with Yahoo as product manager. Later he started his own company, Louder Design. His creativity gave birth to his current successful business, Gruv Gear where he is the president and chief designer.

Our prayer that he would someday serve the Lord is being answered today as he serves God in church, in his home, and through his company. He also encourages and inspires his wife and sons to serve the Lord.

CCBC, A BRIEF INTERLUDE

Two months after I left Campus Crusade, Brother Ric Jumawan recruited me to serve at Capitol City Baptist Church (CCBC). He was the same man who owned the RBJ Building at the University Belt, who challenged me to fill the second floor of his building with people when I was with Crusade. He asked me to fill the vacancy at CCBC left open by the former pastor who went to the U.S. for further studies, and I happened to be available at that time. The pastor that was left behind, Pastor Dan Bautista, oversaw the Tagalog congregation.

My time at CCBC was short-lived. I only served for 12 months. The highlights of my ministry with the church were starting the Homebuilders' Club and leading the Thursday Bible class.

The **Homebuilders' Club** was a once-a-month event specifically for married couples which included parlor games and a lively discussion on topics such as parenting, finances, and husband-wife relationship, to name a few. The meeting usually ended with a time of fellowship and refreshment. It was held at the home of Mr. and Mrs. Romulo Petines on Times Street, West Triangle, Quezon City.

The **Thursday Bible class** which I led for a time, was started by a dedicated couple, Percy and Priscilla Damazo. It was also hosted by Mr. Romulo Petines, who happened to be Priscilla's uncle. Those who attended regularly were Rene and Stella Atienza, John and Lulu Planas, Nelson and Ching Petines, Deng and Sucel Samonte, Eddie and Thelma Ilagan, and Eden Bañez, a friend and co-worker of the Damazos. Pastor Dan Bautista and his wife Norma also came and taught the class from time to time. Little did I know that out of the class, most would go into full-time ministry.

Rene Atienza served in various capacities such as CBAP General Director and Evangelism Explosion Director for Asia. John Planas became a pastor in Hayward, California. Nelson Petines became CCBC Church Administrator and later served as Chairman of CB PACT (Plant-A-Church-Together). Deng and Sucel Samonte became missionaries to Bangladesh and Eden Bañez served as a volunteer worker at the First Evangelical Free Church in Fullerton, CA, where Chuck Swindoll was pastor. Dan Bautista continued at CCBC and later migrated to Canada. He currently pastors a church in Surrey, Canada.

When I left CCBC to lead the association of churches (CBAP), Tony Pezzotta, a former Catholic priest, took over as teacher of the Thursday class. Whenever opportunities arose, I still joined the class up to the time we left the country. At this writing, Tony had gone home to his reward since April 2014.

OPERATION 200

While still pastoring at CCBC, I received a new challenge from Ric Jumawan. He was then board chairman of the church and at the same time, president of CBAP.

A New Challenge

He said, "Your gifts, personality, and leadership style fit the association's needs. Will you consider moving from the pastorate to serving as a denominational leader?" After hearing more about the association's needs and potential for growth, and praying about it, I accepted the challenge.

On July 4, 1976, I was installed as Executive Director (later called General Director) of CBAP and Director of Operation 200, together with Jake Toews as O-200 Associate Director. O-200 was the association's goal of planting 200 churches with 10,000 baptized believers in ten years' time. This came about

"Let's work together to fulfill O-200"

because of a survey conducted by Leonard Tuggy of Conservative Baptist Foreign Mission Society (now known as WorldVenture), Ralph Toliver of Overseas Missionary Fellowship (OMF), and Gordon Swanson of Far Eastern Gospel Crusade (now known as Send International). The survey revealed that churches around the country had an average of 50 members. Tuggy concluded that if CBAP planted 200 churches with 50 members in each church, there would be 10,000 members in a span of 10 years. The program was officially adopted by the association in 1971, and it was set from 1972 to 1981. The first leaders who became involved with O-200 were Rev. David Yount and evangelist Paul Mortiz.

By the way, what Ric Jumawan did not say when he challenged me was that CBAP didn't have enough funds to run its current programs. It didn't even have its own office but only shared with the mission office, occupying the second floor of a building on West Avenue, and the only way to the CBAP office was to pass through the mission office. The CBAP office was a conference room with an oversized round table in the middle and two small rooms used by two secretaries: Dory Baldeo for CBAP and Normi Garcia for Operation 200.

New Strategy

CBAP was halfway through the O-200 program when I came in. At that time there were 53 churches and chapels with four full-time church planters namely: Luis Notario (Riverside Mills Corporation, Rosario, Pasig), Joseph Jimenez (Manggahan, Pasig), Sergio

Velasquez (Imus, Cavite), and Abe Luis (Bolinao, Pangasinan).

The fundraising slogan was *"Piso Bawa't Miembro"* (One Peso per Member) and each church had a coordinator who collected the pesos from the members. These coordinators met every month at the CBAP office to give updates and submit their collection.

RBJ rallying others to get involved

We had an O-200 theme song, written by Russell Maningas, a CBAP member:

> *"Tayo ay magkaisa, mga CBAP, magsikap*
> *upang matupad*
> *Ang layuning pinapangarap, 200 churches*
> *ay maitatag.*
> *Panginoon, kami'y tulungan, sa gawain*
> *Mo'y magtagumpay*
> *Pangunahan sa aming bawa't hakbang*
> *At kami'y bigyan Mong kasiglahan."*

Roughly translated, the song said, "Let us unite, CBAP members, strive to fulfill our dream of reaching 200 churches. Help us, Lord, to succeed in Your work; guide our steps and give us enthusiasm."

There was a shift of emphasis from 200 churches of 50 members to fewer churches but more members.

Fifty members could hardly support a pastor but perhaps 70 to 80 could do better.

In the meantime, we underwent some adjustment of strategy and realignment of personnel. Abe Luis was recalled from Pangasinan to serve as music personnel. We moved northward with CCBC sending Ting Ardina as church planter to Muñoz, Nueva Ecija and Cabanatuan City. A professional tennis player and instructor, his qualifications opened doors for him to meet several contacts.

"Pag-aani '77"

"Pag-aani '77" (Harvest '77) was held in San Jose, Nueva Ecija, in conjunction with the Programmed Evangelism project of Conservative Baptist Bible College (CBBC). It was a two-week nightly evangelistic meeting at the town plaza. During the day, visits to various homes were made by students. One of the fruits of the campaign was Vice Mayor Manolo Tan. A small group of believers continued meeting after the campaign under the leadership of Pastor Ardina, who now moved to San Jose.

In 1978, we sent church planters to Nueva Vizcaya and Isabela (Hermenegildo Ulat in Bayombong, Rudy Basto in Solano, and Pedro Bernardo in Cauayan, Isabela). We held nightly campaigns in these towns with Roger Baldemor as the main speaker.

The plan was to start churches along the pan-Philippine highway from Cagayan Province up north to Davao in Mindanao in the south. We also surveyed the Bicol region, particularly Naga City.

A church near San Jose, California, had a policy that whenever they put up a new building on their property, they would set aside an amount for missions specifically for a church building. San Jose, Nueva Ecija, became the recipient of this mission project from the First Baptist Church of Los Altos, a city near San Jose, California.

New Territories

As the number of church planters increased, many churches took the challenge of supporting the church planting program in several cities and towns. The year 1979 saw the beginning of work among the cultural minorities (Aetas) in Zambales. At the same time, Mindanao Mission was started with the arrival of Bob Skivington, who just finished his postgraduate studies at Fuller School of World Mission. His Doctor of Missiology project about a new strategy for starting churches would now be implemented in the south based on the book he published—*Mission to Mindanao.*

Before the culmination of O-200, churches, pastors, and missionaries felt the urgency of doubling the church planting efforts. Extra push was made to reach the O-200 goal, though its focus was on the number of baptized believers rather than the number of churches. Additional works were opened in the provinces of Oriental Mindoro, Camarines Sur, La Union, Zambales, Nueva Viscaya, Isabela, and Negros Occidental, among others.

"Pista ng Papuri"

At the "Pista ng Papuri" (Festival of Praise) celebration on November 30, 1981, held at the Philippine

International Convention Center (PICC), the total reported number of baptized believers was 10,245. Our former missionary, Abe Luis, conducted a 250-voice choir representing most of the CBAP churches. It was a great day of exaltation and praise to our God!

We did not reach the goal of 200 churches (we counted 118 churches and chapels) but the number of baptized believers totaled 10,245 surpassing the goal by 245. That meant instead of having an average of 50 people in a church, it went up to 87 in weekly attendance. With that number, a church was in a better position to support a pastor than with only 50 members. The rationale was to increase our strength rather than our weakness, and this was the focus of our next major program.

Pictured here with Gladys, Jake served as O-200 Associate Director then Church Planting Director

While rejoicing over the success of O-200, a more ambitious program was launched dubbed "Harvest 20,000," which was to double the number of members in four years! Dare we dream and attempt greater things for God? Yes, and Amen!

THE CAMPING PROGRAM

The camping program played a vital part in the growth of churches and individuals, especially among the youth. In fact, even before the association was organized, there were already summer youth camps led by missionaries and pastors of some local churches. The first youth camp that I ever attended when I was in high school was held near Baguio City and was sponsored by different mission groups.

As more churches got together to form CBAP, it became apparent that a strong camping program was needed. Association-wide summer camps were led by missionaries, pastors, and Bible school students and graduates. Dr. and Mrs. William Simons, Don and Alice Benson, Beulah Heaton, Rosalinda Ison (Ferguson), Nelly Gonzales (Rebong), Flor Alvarez (Baldemor), Nelida Presbitero (Lacaba), and Roger Baldemor were among the first camp organizers and leaders.

In the beginning, youth camps were held in places such as Kaliraya in Lumban, Laguna, at Jamboree Site in Mount Makiling, Los Baños, Laguna, and at Twin Rocks, Balayan Bay in Anilao, Batangas. Later, Villa Sylvia in Nagcarlan, Laguna, became a more permanent campsite.

Villa Sylvia

The leadership made a deal with the owners of Villa Sylvia. Over a period of 20 years, we would develop the site and build some structures, in exchange for our exclusive use of the place 16 weeks out of each year. Camps were held for junior high age, third- and fourth-year high school students, college-age young people, and pastors' families.

Pastor Pantoja (left) & Pastor Paulme

Villa Sylvia became the venue for important events like fellowship rallies and mass baptisms. In 1977, CBAP members gathered there for a memorable occasion: the honorary ordination of two of the oldest pastors of the association, in recognition of their faithful service for many years. They were Pastor Luis Pantoja, Sr. and Pastor Paulino Paulme.

The camps were planned and led by the Christian Education personnel like Norma Presbitero (Bautista), Rowena Valdecantos (Balquiedra), and Ofelia Dave (Ilardo). Other members of the camp planning committee were Dan Pantoja and Sonny Vitaliz, who also served as speakers.

Changed Lives

It would not be easy to measure the impact of the camps on the lives of both staff and campers. Suffice it to say that there were a lot of changed lives. Several young people prayed to receive Christ, many were assured of their salvation, and some received confirmation of their call to serve God, notably Susan Bagcus who became a missionary to Thailand.

Here are some testimonies.

> It was in May 1972, when I was just 13 years old, I attended a youth camp at Villa Sylvia Resort in Nagcarlan, Laguna.
>
> Since childhood, I had heard so much about Jesus Christ who sacrificed his life and shed His blood on the cross for the forgiveness of my sins. It was the camp speaker, Mr. Tony Reyes, however, who shared a message entitled "Credo: The Love of God," that challenged me. He stressed the point that God gives eternal life to those who believe. When Pastor Reyes asked who among us campers would like to receive Christ, I raised my hand to
>
>
>
> indicate the most important decision I've ever made. It was a real turning point in my life. Since then, the Holy Spirit has helped me overcome my weaknesses and guided me towards the renewing of my mind. He led me to embrace a new set of values. My first camp attendance was for free, but I saved my own

money to join the youth camp the following year which was also held in Villa Sylvia. That time I decided to serve the Lord for the rest of my life.

It's been proven several times, and I have personally witnessed it, that many people make major decisions during their adolescent years. I believe that chemistry has not changed. Youth with a lot of questions in their minds may get a lot of different answers. Yet, gathering them intentionally in camp shall give them one ultimate answer that can change their outlook in life—the Lord Jesus Christ.

I was saved in camp and dedicated my life to full-time ministry in camp. I have served in many capacities at camp. Now, I am even more focused on the ministry of camp. I encourage our local churches to make camping ministry a high priority.

Jerry Olarte
Global Ministries
Pastor, Highland Baptist Church
Westminster, Colorado, USA

∧∧∧∧∧

As a teenager, I became friends with some young people who were studying the Bible. They invited me to go with them to a camp for high school students in Balayan, Batangas. My brother, Thelmo, and I went with them. There at camp I met many youths from Laguna, Quezon, and Manila. Our counselors and group study leaders were Bible school students including Olre Presbitero, Lina Bautista (Baldemor), and others. There at Twin Rocks in Balayan, I finally understood what Christ had done for me at the cross. I accepted Him into my heart as my Lord and Savior.

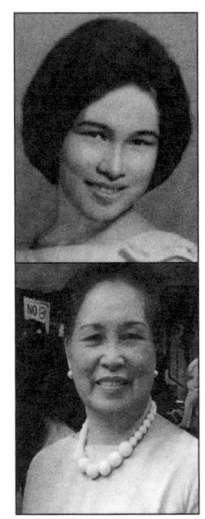

When we returned to Tanauan, I became active in the church. As I began to mature in Christ, I had the privilege of teaching children's Sunday School. Today as an adult, I have served in various ways like leading the women's ministry and acting as adviser to the current women's leaders. I'm married to Manuel Lascano, who is a leader in our church. Our four children are also serving the Lord.

I thank God for using that camp so many years ago to bring me to Himself!

Chit Alcantara-Lascano
Women's Ministry Adviser
Tanauan Bible Church
Tanuaun, Batangas, Philippines

∧∧∧∧∧

At a young age, I became exposed to the CBAP camping ministry when I first attended camp in Batangas in the summer of 1962. My camp counselor was Pastor Ernie Montealegre, while the camp speaker was Pastor Leo Calica.

I attended the youth camp almost every year until I reached high school when other interests vied for my attention.

It was then that I got involved in acting in school plays. At my high school graduation, I received the Best Actor award which prompted my guidance counselor to encourage me to pursue a career in acting. I auditioned at ABS-CBN and was accepted to join a drama group that staged plays in the provinces. My director, Orly Ilacad, even gave me a stage name, "Butch Castro."

In the summer of 1970, I was scheduled to perform in Palawan with the drama group. I was given an allowance to buy clothes for the play and for other things that I might need. A few days before my trip I stayed in the home of my sister and brother-in-law, Lynn and Oscar Baldemor.

Then I heard that there was going to be a youth camp in Los Baños, Laguna, the same week as my Palawan trip. I wanted to go and be with my camp friends, but I also struggled because going with the drama group meant I would have a good chance to pursue my acting dream. That night I had a long talk with God. He was so good. He gave me peace in my heart to go to the camp.

I called my manager and told him about my struggle and my decision. He was very understanding and gave me his blessings. He even said not to worry about the allowance; consider it a gift to me.

When I headed for camp the following, morning, my sister and brother-in-law were very happy for the answer to my prayer.

That week at camp, the messages seemed to be personally directed to me. The speaker asked, "What will you do with your life? Whom will you serve?" When he challenged the campers to give their lives to Jesus to serve Him full-time, I went forward and dedicated my life to serve the Lord. I realized He called me to be a pastor, not an actor.

When school opened, I enrolled at FEBIAS College of Bible. In 1975, I completed my Bachelor of Arts degree in Bible and Theology.

Following my graduation, I served as associate pastor at Capitol City Baptist Church. During our time at CCBC, my wife Norma and I continued to be involved in organizing, planning, and working with the youth camps, a ministry that we enjoyed for many years. To God be the glory!

Dan Bautista
Pastor, Jesus, Our Rock Christian Church
Surrey, British Columbia, Canada

The camping program utilized the expertise of leaders and other personnel. It helped the Bible school students to mature as they accepted the challenge of counseling and leading young people in devotions and group Bible study.

PASTORS' FAMILY CAMP

One of the significant and memorable activities of the association's camping program was the Pastors' Family Camp. Held every summer at Villa Sylvia, Nagcarlan, Laguna, it brought together CBAP pastors and their families for one week of fun, fellowship, relaxation, and just a change of pace and atmosphere from their regular ministry schedule. Dr. William Simons, whom everyone called "Dad" by now, made it his personal project to raise funds for this yearly gathering. We all looked forward to this opportunity to be with co-workers and enjoy one another amid God's beautiful creation. Pastors' families from the cities and the provinces considered it a real treat to be at family camp.

Most pastors did not have the means to go on a family vacation. The camp allowed everyone to get away at a minimum expense. One reason we were able to do this was because the camp staff, notably the kitchen crew, was composed of volunteers from the churches. They did the shopping for food, cooking, serving, and cleaning up for free.

Aside from an undivided time of fellowship, the camp was an opportunity to build relationships with co-workers from different churches. We encouraged one another, sharing highs and lows not only in the ministry but also in our personal lives. We were able to voice concerns and other issues, without being afraid that what was shared would later haunt us.

An important benefit of the Pastors' Family Camp was its effect on the children. They realized that they were not alone: other "PKs" (Pastors' Kids), whether from the city or the province, dealt with the same issues of people's expectations of them. After camping, these kids stayed in touch with each other, developing life-long friendships that they continued to treasure.

As a pastor, what I liked most was being part of a bigger family. If a member was moving to another location, we could recommend them to a church whose pastor we met at family camp.

The daily schedule at camp was simple: morning and evening devotions were led by selected campers. The rest of the day was spent playing and having friendly competitions and age-appropriate activities for the children, teenagers, and adults. Those who did not feel like participating in group games and sports spent time reading, meditating, or exploring the campsite by themselves or with some friends. The meals were always sumptuous, with fruits, vegetables, meat, and fish, purchased fresh from the nearby market and prepared by our volunteer kitchen crew.

The highlight of the camp was the last day which we called "fiesta" or festival. It featured special games like *Juego de Anillo* (Game of Rings), *Palo Sebo* (Climbing a slippery bamboo pole to reach the prize on top), and other races and relays. The dinner was special, complete with delicious food and the traditional lechon (whole roast pig). Then the campers who were divided into teams competed in an impromptu talent show of songs, dances, and skits.

Truly, Pastors' Family Camp was one way that CBAP "took care of our own."

The last night was always fun!

THE ROLE OF MASS MEDIA

In 1978, Lynn was appointed as editor of the Baptist Messenger, the official newsletter of the association. Its purpose was to disseminate relevant information on the progress of the current program and what was happening in the different churches.

Baptist Messenger

Almost every month we would send out copies of these newsletters to all the churches through different means. Pastors, missionaries, student workers, and other CBAP members who came to the office willingly carried bundles of the Baptist Messenger to their churches. Sometimes we mailed them out. We also had a mailing list of individual CBAP members and prayer partners who lived abroad. That way we maintained our connection with our constituency. We shared not only news of events and accomplishments but also prayer concerns. As churches learned of current developments, they faithfully prayed for and supported the association financially.

The Baptist Messenger was an integral part of CBAP since it was the main link between the national office and the member churches. We didn't have today's modern technology, but it served the purpose.

Radio Programs

The challenge of staying connected was further augmented by our weekly radio program over DZAS: the "O-200 Hour" and later "Programang Harvest 20,000." Even people in far-flung areas were reached by radio and were kept abreast of the association's news and happenings. We knew people were listening because we got regular feedback from them. Those involved in the production were Lynn Baldemor (script writer), Pastor Dan Bautista (emcee and devotional speaker), and Cheryl Marquez (news round-up). Occasionally, Pastor Joe Arceo took his turn to speak. We also played a song or two to liven up the program.

Cheryl Marquez (Zamora) and a guest speaker at the radio praogram taping

TV Specials

We had the opportunity to even use television to spread the Gospel message. Back in 1984, the Rev. Fred Magbanua, Managing Director of Far East Broadcasting Company (FEBC), served as President of CBAP. At the same time, he was a member of Kapisanan ng mga Brodkaster sa Pilipinas (KBP) and the Broadcast Media Council (BMC).

One day, he came to the office, all excited. He just came from the BMC meeting, where one of the things they talked about was the need for quality television shows during Holy Week. Every year they aired old religious films like "Quo Vadiz," "Ten Commandments," and "Ben Hur," or they simply closed "in solemn observation of the Lenten Season." Fred had a sudden inspiration. He asked his broadcast colleagues, "If someone could produce a TV special for Holy Week, would you show it for free on prime time?" They said, "Yes!" So, he went straight to our office and said, "Let's produce a TV special."

We put our heads together—Rene Atienza, our Promotions Director, Lynn, our resident writer, and me—and brainstormed the project. We decided to title our TV special, *"Naiibang Biernes Santo"* ("A Different Kind of Good Friday"). It would run for 90 minutes and include testimonies, songs, a puppet skit, a question-and-answer segment about Good Friday practices and beliefs, and a very short message. Our inspiration was the then popular "700 Club." We would also include a response mechanism so people could write to us, ask questions, or give comments, and send for the free literature that we were offering.

On a limited time (less than two months before Holy Week) and an even more limited budget (as in zero), we went to work. From among CB churches, we found three individuals to share their testimonies, two choirs, a trio, two soloists, and three people to form the panel for the question and answer. There were also two puppeteers from a children's show similar to Sesame Street who wrote the script for their segment. I prepared a short message.

How about the production staff? And the equipment? Rev. Magbanua borrowed cameras and camera men from his friend, Rev. Eddie Villanueva (Jesus is Lord ministry). A crew member from Channel 7 helped us with lights and sound. After three straight days of shooting came editing and other details and soon, our TV special was ready to roll!

When Good Friday came that year, television audiences watched "Naiibang Biernes Santo" on Channels 4, 9, and 13. After the message, we invited people to write if they had any questions. We also offered a free booklet, *"Sino ang Dios?"* ("Who is God?"). We received a lot of letters!

Greatly encouraged, we dared to produce two more TV specials: *"Naiibang Kalayaan"* (A Different Kind of Freedom), for Independence Day and *"Naiibang Pasko"* (A Different Kind of Christmas). Using a similar format as the first one, we invited certain members of CBAP churches to participate. Again, our TV specials were aired on three channels at no cost to us!

Then the Lord led us to venture into drama for television. For two consecutive years we produced original dramas that were shown during Holy Week. The first one was "To Live Again" starring Rosa Rosal who was then a member of Greenhills Christian Fellowship and the second one was "No Greater Love" with Tirso Cruz III as the leading character. He was then attending Congregation of Fishers of Men at BF Homes in Parañaque.

These two were the only professionals that appeared in our dramas. The rest were from our churches in Metro Manila who were willing to act and needed very little coaching: Sharon Clavecilla, Rhea Chanco, Fe Tarroja, Esther Flor Baldemor, Lito Gonzales, Celine Baldemor, Fred and Aliw Magbanua, Gideon Gaitano,

Caren Sison, and Noel Pantoja, to name a few. By the way, Rosa Rosal and Tirso Cruz III did not ask for any talent fee; they just accepted a little love gift from us. The rest of the cast and crew were treated to dinner. I think we might have started the trend in low-budget filmmaking! Ross Tarroja and Lynn Baldemor directed the dramas with the help and advice of Marcial Sanson, a legendary television director who had become a Christian (he used to direct the long-running series, "*Gulong ng Palad*"). By the way, the dramas had English titles, but the dialogues were mostly in Tagalog. The stories were also based on real-life situations with Biblical applications and a Gospel presentation, but were not preachy at all!

We probably would have produced more TV programs had we not left for the U.S.

TRAVELS

When I was based in the Philippines, I had opportunities to represent the organization I was working with at different international meetings.

International Conferences

In July 1974, when I was with Campus Crusade, I was its lone delegate to the International Congress on World Evangelization in Lausanne, Switzerland. I traveled in a chartered plane with more than one hundred Filipino Christian leaders. The most significant thing that I learned and observed was the acknowledgement of the shift of Christianity's center of gravity from the western world to Africa, Asia, and Latin America.

From Lausanne, I met up with the Philippine delegation to Explo '74 in Seoul, South Korea, the following month. Explo '74 was attended by approximately 300,000 delegates. Police officially estimated a crowd of 1.5 million at one of the evening meetings.

Visits to the U.S.

During my term as General Director of CBAP, I had several opportunities to visit the United States as a guest of our American brethren. I spoke in regional conferences, shared my testimony on what the Lord was doing in the Philippines, and gave messages on various occasions. Some local churches invited me to share in their mission conferences.

"My name is Oscar Baldemor. I am a product of missionary endeavors in the Philippines." This is usually how I would introduce myself wherever I was asked to speak. Then I would recount how missionaries Dr. and Mrs. William Simons, Miss Beulah Heaton, and others first came to my hometown and introduced Jesus Christ to my family. I shared about the beginnings of the association and how it had grown to where the leadership was now mostly composed of nationals.

My travels brought me to the length and breadth of the United States, where I met fellow Christians who were eager to know more about mission work in the Philippines. I spoke both at big city churches and very small country churches that even used their courtyards as cemeteries for their departed members!

Some folks were curious about Filipinos and asked me sincere questions, like, "What kind of food do you eat?", "Do some of your people still live in trees?", "Do your children watch television?"

In one of the regional meetings on the East Coast, one of the delegates came up to me while I was seated on the front pew and asked, "Do you speak English?" in a rather loud voice. I thought I would have some fun with him, so I replied, "Huh?" He repeated himself, this time his voice was louder. He spoke more slowly, and used deliberate hand gestures, and said, "Do...you...speak...

English?" Again, I answered, "Huh?" He tried again and when I gave the same answer, he left me alone, obviously frustrated.

I was the main speaker that night, and of course, I gave the message in English. Right after the service, he came to me and said, "You rascal!" Then he good-naturedly conversed with me for a few minutes.

Some of the perks of traveling as a guest included meeting members of the local churches and interacting with them, staying in some of their homes and being driven to and from meetings. Occasionally, these new friends took me sightseeing.

Honorary Doctorates

One highlight of my travels was my special "visit" to Denver Seminary in Colorado on June 4, 1983. The reason: They awarded me with a Doctor of Divinity degree, Honoris Causa, in recognition of my role in the fulfillment of Operation 200. It was both a humbling and elating experience.

Together with my wife, I sat in the sanctuary of Riverside Baptist Church where the commencement took place, amazed and grateful for God's goodness. Dr. Haddon Robinson, the seminary president, placed the hood on me. What a unique honor!

At Denver Seminary, accepting my honorary doctoral degree

A week later on June 11, California School of Theology conferred on me a Doctor of Humane Letters degree. It was a pleasant surprise.

Gifts for New Church Buildings

While visiting a church in Los Altos, California, I was able to raise money for the church in San Jose, Nueva Ecija, to build their own place of worship.

In 1981, after speaking at a church in Oregon, an 88-year-old gentleman came up to me after the service. He said that he would like to donate some money to missions, to perpetuate his wife's memory who had recently passed away. Is there a church in the Philippines that could use that money? I immediately thought of the Bayombong, Nueva Vizcaya church that was looking to buy their own property but did not have the funds for it. That gentleman was so pleased to help and today there's a plaque on the wall of the church in Bayombong that says:

> "This building was constructed on September 15, 1982, through the combined efforts of the Bayombong Baptist Church and CB Pact, with a generous financial assistance of Mr. William Seamster of Oregon City, Oregon, U.S.A. in memory of his beloved wife, the late Diane Seamster. Dedicated this 16th day of January in the year of our Lord nineteen hundred and eighty-three."

Lastly, my travels enabled me to meet with missionary candidates who were eager to know more about the

Philippines. It was a privilege to help them affirm their vision and call. Several of them came and spent their whole missionary career in my country.

HARVEST 20,000

Harvest 20,000 was the new program to double CBAP's membership from 10,000 to 20,000 in four years' time, from 1982 to 1985. The situation at this time was quite different from when I took over the helm of O-200. With the former, we were several thousand behind, whereas when we started Harvest 20,000, we were more than two hundred baptized believers ahead. So, we plotted out our next move to continue growth while our people were still in high spirits to move on. We recruited more church planters and encouraged individual churches to help plant more churches.

New Plan of Partnership

At this point, the former Joint Work Program (JWP) between the association and the mission agency was ended and a new plan of partnership was initiated. Instead of committees, the CBAP national office was restructured to be composed of the General Director, Director of Training, Director for Church Development, Director for Church Planting, and Director for Promotions.

Associated Gospel Churches

One significant development was when Associated Gospel Churches (AGC) joined CBAP which bolstered our reaching 20,000 members.

AGC, headed by Rev. Leo del Carmen, was based in Cauayan, Negros Occidental. Rev. del Carmen also initiated the founding of Isio Private Academy and Berean Bible Institute, also located in Isio, Cauayan, Negros Occidental. When his health started to fail and no successor was in sight, it was suggested that AGC should affiliate with another like-minded organization for continuity should something happen to Pastor del Carmen.

AGC had already planted several churches in cooperation with an organization called Luke Society, Inc., a group of physicians and dentists within the Christian Reformed Church U.S.A. It was started in the Philippines in response to medical needs in Negros Occidental. Based in Bacolod City, Luke Society was engaged in establishing medical clinics, community development, and community health, resulting in the planting of churches. Dr. Russell Atonson and his wife, Glenda, Pastor del Carmen's daughter and son-in-law, headed the Philippine team from 1980 to 1998.

Rev. Leo del Carmen and Pastor Donnie Friolo connected AGC with Rev. Fred Magbanua who was then the president of CBAP. These three gentlemen were all from Cauayan town.

At the CBAP annual conference in Baguio City on November 28, 1985, a total of 25 AGC churches were accepted as members of the association. They were represented by Rev. Proferio Alcala, director of Isio Private Academy, Dr. Russell Atonson, director of Luke Society and his wife, Glenda, and the pastors of the churches. These churches were scattered in the towns of Cauayan, Ilog, Kabankalan, Sipalay, Hinobaan, Dumaguete, Bacolod, Hinigaran, Himamaylan, and in towns of Quezon and Rizal in the province of Palawan.

A New Thrust

In 1986, missionary Bo Horlen and his wife Cynthia moved from Mindanao to open the CB work in Cebu. He ministered there until 2008. During that time frame he saw 24 churches planted in Negros, Cebu, Leyte, and some other smaller islands.

At the end of Harvest 20,000, we overshot the goal by over a thousand. At the second Biennial Conference in Baguio City, the leadership took another step of faith and asked God to increase our growth rate to bring the number to 60,000 by the end of 1990, and launched a new thrust, Mission 60,000. A goal of 600 churches was also established to coincide with the 60,000 membership. It means increasing the number of members to an average of 100 per church.

It was in the middle of this program that my family and I left for the U.S. A new General Director was appointed to continue leading the association.

MOVE TO THE U.S.

I wanted to pursue my studies but at that time, there was no school in the Philippines offering what I wanted to study: Missions on the postgraduate level. I researched and found out that Fuller Theological Seminary School of World Mission brought leaders from all over the world. So I focused on going to Fuller.

Then I had to think of the details: How would I pay for my school expenses? How would I support my family while I go to school? And where would we live?

I made an agreement with the family that I was not going alone. Either everyone goes or I would not go at all. We didn't want anyone, especially the kids, to be left behind. I had to decide soon because my eldest daughter was already eighteen and her window of opportunity to be included was only three years. I didn't even know how I was going. I didn't know if a student visa would be enough to bring the whole family. At that time, I was not qualified to go on a student visa because I hadn't been accepted yet by Fuller or by any other school.

Surprise Offer

In 1986, I fulfilled my commitment to speak at different churches in the U.S. in my capacity as CBAP General Director. When I got to Northern California, I made a courtesy call to the CB association director in the region, Dr. Bruce Clatterbuck. I shared my vision with him and my desire to pursue my postgraduate studies at Fuller in Pasadena. I didn't know that Dr. Mark Platt, Dr. Clatterbuck's associate, and church planting director was a Fuller alumnus and an adjunct faculty at the Fuller School of World Mission (now called Fuller School of Intercultural Studies), the very school where I wanted to enroll.

Dr. Clatterbuck got excited at the prospect of my coming. He shared with me that he wanted to strengthen the ethnic ministry in his region. He said that with a student visa, my work opportunities were limited. I would not be able to work outside of the school and it would be part-time. He then gave me a proposal: "If you're willing to help us in the ethnic ministry, we're willing to sponsor you as an immigrant under the non-quota Religious Worker's visa." I could not believe what I just heard. Such a generous offer! I was excited but I tried not to show it. I agreed to his proposal on the condition that my ministry with them would be for only one year. It meant delaying my enrollment at Fuller.

A few days later, I went to see an immigration lawyer in San Francisco for me to fill out the necessary papers to apply for a Religious Worker's visa with my wife and four children as dependents. I was surprised that the lawyer only charged me $500 for a family of six instead of charging us per person. He told me that our visas would be processed at the U.S. Embassy in Manila. All I needed to do was wait for them to notify me. So I went back to the Philippines wondering when I would hear from them.

U.S. Embassy

One rainy July day, a partially wet package showed up in our mailbox. I didn't know what it was. I carefully opened it. To my surprise, it was a response from the U.S. Embassy. It said, "Your application has been approved." It went on to say that they wanted me to schedule an interview before the end of the year; the earlier, the better. I was surprised and excited at the same time.

There was one problem though, since there were six of us in the family, I needed to pay $125.00 for each visa. I was earning in pesos, not in dollars.

Our interview was scheduled for August 14, 1987. We were told to come in at 8:30 a.m. The kids missed school. We sat there waiting to be called. When 12 o'clock came, they instructed us to have lunch and come back at 1:00 pm.

We were assigned to a consul who had a reputation of being quite strict. When we finally faced her, she said, "You didn't have to bring your kids." Then she reviewed our application and noted that it said, "Religious Worker" and told me, "We need someone like you to teach people in America about God." After saying that, she stamped our passports and told me, "You're approved. You must leave in four months." She added, "If for some reason you're not able to leave within that period, you must start the process all over again. I advise you to think of leaving by December 14."

There was a problem. The kids were in school. My son was scheduled to graduate from Quezon City

Science High School at the end of March. I was supposed to graduate with my Master of Divinity degree from the Asian Theological Seminary in the same month. My eldest daughter had to finish the semester at UP. I explained all this to the consul and asked for a reconsideration. To my surprise, she gave us another four months: leave by April 14, no further extension. That whole thing was a series of surprises: first, Clatterbuck's offer to sponsor the family; second, getting approved after only six months from the time we applied; third, receiving an extension on our departure date.

Resigned

In a January 1988 CBAP council meeting, I officially resigned as CBAP General Director after serving for 12 years. The council, headed by the Bishop Fred Magbanua, understood my desire, and made a counter offer: "Take an extended study leave of absence and resume your position as General Director when you come back."

It was a tempting offer. It made me feel "important," but I thought it was not a good move for the association. It was also not good for the person who would take my place. So, I politely turned down the offer. I chose to resign completely. The person to take over my place needed to be secure in his position. After much deliberation, the council finally accepted my resignation. They said, "Your resignation will be effective on the day you leave the country."

The next major hurdle was purchasing plane tickets for six people. Our small savings were depleted from embassy fees and medical exams. We had only lived four years in the house that we built in 1984. We thought that was our last move, that our kids would grow up there, that we would live there until we retired, etc., but now we had to move again. Who would stay in our house? My brother and his family agreed to live there since they were getting ready to build their own house on the next lot.

To be able to raise money for our trip, we had to sell our belongings. The amount that we raised was enough to purchase six one-way tickets. The only money in my pocket was $500, CBAP's parting gift.

On Bataan Day, April 9, 1988, missionary Jim Davis drove our family to the airport. With our 12 pieces of luggage and *balikbayan* boxes, our entire worldly possessions, we said goodbye to the friends and relatives who saw us off. Northwest Airlines made a brief stop in Japan. We resumed our flight and after 12 hours, we landed at San Francisco International Airport. Bruce Clatterbuck and our longtime friend and CBAP co-worker, Ric Jumawan were there to greet us.

New Adventure

We had not even claimed our luggage when Bruce took me aside and said, "Welcome to America, Oscar. Here's your first check." It was $3,000, for a job that I had agreed to do but hadn't started yet: Ethnic Ministry Director!

Enter Ric Jumawan. He told me, "I moved to a new house, but I rented my old house for you." The house was semi-furnished but still quite empty so our family spent the night at Clatterbucks' house in San Jose, except for our son, Jay, who couldn't wait to be with his best friend, Ric Jumawan's son, Bong, so he slept over at their house. The following day we moved into our very first house in America: 741 Central Avenue, Alameda, California.

A few days later, we received a call from the mother of Ray Prigodich, a former missionary to the Philippines. Mrs. Adele Prigodich was in her 80s and about to move to a retirement home. What was she going to do with her things? She did not want to have an estate sale. Instead, when she found out that "Ray's former colleague, Oscar Baldemor, and family had just arrived," she decided to give her things to us. She called her children who lived in different parts of the States and asked them if she could do that (after all, that's the house where they grew up; those were their "stuff"). Their answer, "Mom, go for it!"

We were excited that we didn't have to purchase anything. The only concern was how to transport everything from San Jose to Alameda, about an hour's drive each way. Ric Jumawan to the rescue!

He said, "Oscar, my nephew agreed to lend you his truck." The next day, the nephew changed his mind. Ric was very upset. He called and asked me to meet him at the car dealership. "I'm buying a truck that you can use. You can break in this truck for me."

My son and I made several trips for two days to haul a living room set, a dining room set, China cabinets, several bedroom sets, kitchen utensils, dishes, linens, even plants! As newcomers to the U.S., we didn't have a car. Someone loaned me a car— a Reliant that tended to turn left. My friend, Ric, was not too happy. He called me and said, "I'm not comfortable seeing you drive a salvaged vehicle. I'm at Mitsubishi dealership right now, looking at a brand-new Galant like the one you drove in the Philippines. I just need you to come and sign the papers. I'll be your co-borrower." It wasn't hard to persuade me.

In front of 741 Central Avenue during our first Christmas in the U.S.

Fil-Am Bible Church

At that time, there was a new church that Ric and his friends started. Fil-Am Bible Church in Alameda was considered a church plant so helping them was within my responsibility as ethnic ministry director. They were renting facilities at the Veterans' building for Sunday school classes and worship service.

I agreed to be interim pastor of Fil-Am, making it clear that I would eventually move to Southern California for my studies. My commitment was up to the end of the year. Even though I knew I wasn't staying in Alameda for long, I served as if I was—conducting home Bible studies and leading the small group of believers. I also baptized 12 people. By this time, I was already accepted at Fuller Seminary but I still didn't have the finances to go to school and support my family. The monthly check from CB Northern California was going to stop when we moved to Southern California. I needed a miracle!

Scholarship

One day, I got a call from a man named Dennis Baker. He said, "I understand that you're going to help Bethany Church in Long Beach start a Filipino congregation. I have referred you to a guy named Don M. He has a foundation that supports seminary students on the graduate level. Who was Dennis Baker? Why was he willing to help me? And what about Bethany?

Then I remembered that when we were still in the Philippines, I got a call from Pastor Matt Hannan, Executive Pastor of Bethany Church in Long Beach, inviting me to help them start a Filipino church. Without even realizing where Long Beach was in relation to Fuller where I was headed, I sort of agreed to help. Our first long drive as a family was from Alameda to Long Beach to meet with the leadership of Bethany.

We also met some members of the church who made us feel at home. The senior pastor, Dennis Beatty, and his family, came to our room at the Holiday Inn to welcome us, bringing a box of donuts. The following day, another family, the Souders, treated us to lunch after church at a restaurant by the beach.

We did not meet Dennis Baker at that time, but he knew we were in town. I learned later that he was the General Director of the Southern California association of churches.

The Lord used him to deliver the miracle for my going to Fuller by connecting me to the Don M. Foundation. "Oscar," he said to me during that fateful phone conversation, "Don is waiting for your call." So, I called.

Mr. Don M. told me that he would send someone to bring me an application form that I was to fill out in front of his representative. The following day, his son-in-law was at our door. I filled out the application with all the pertinent details including how much I would need to pay for my schooling and support my family. The following day, I received a call that I was approved! What a surprise. They committed to support me for four years.

New Home

The next surprise was how God provided a house for us to rent. Bethany Church promised to pay for our housing while I started a Filipino church. We concentrated our house-hunting in the Long Beach area. Within one day, we found a three-bedroom bungalow, signed the contract, and gave a security deposit. It was in West Long Beach, which we learned later, was home to a lot of Filipinos! We had no idea, but the Lord knew exactly where we needed to be.

There I was, getting ready to go to school full-time, church-planting among my *"kababayans"* (countrymen) in a new country, and raising a young family. The commute between Long Beach and Pasadena was at least 45 minutes each way. Long before we knew that it was going to be the distance I would travel, God had already supplied me with a reliable car back when we were still in Alameda.

SOUTHERN CALIFORNIA

On December 29, 1988, early in the morning, with all our earthly possessions packed in a U-Haul, our family started our drive from Northern to Southern California. With us in two other cars were some of our church members from Alameda whom I had baptized earlier. We all celebrated New Year's Eve together. They were quite eager to help us begin our new adventure in faith.

Starting a New Church

At the very onset of starting a new church, I had in mind that I would stay with the church until they owned a property. It was a leap of faith, not knowing that the city of Long Beach had limited space for new church buildings, but I was led to make that commitment.

When Bethany Church challenged me to start a Filipino congregation, one of the leaders told me, "The Filipinos who attend Bethany are waiting for you." I met three of them: Sandie Gan, a Filipino-Chinese single lady, and a couple, Eli and Carmen Smith. The three, plus two sisters, Joy and Jane Galazo, whom we knew from Manila, my wife Lynn, my eldest daughter Celine, and I formed our first Bible class. We met every Saturday night at our home.

Our first Bible class that started Fil-Am Christian Fellowship. Front from left: Jane Galazo & Sandie Gan (Justen). Back row: Celine, Oscarr & Lynn, Carmen & Eli Smith.

Incidentally, we learned that a musician from Bethany Church was going to give free guitar lessons for beginners. Our two teenage kids, Celine and Jay, joined the class. They learned how to play a new song every week and that's what we sang at our home Bible class. This went on for months and the teacher even gave Jay his old guitar. By the way, our son became really good at playing the guitar, and he eventually taught some kids from our church. He himself became part of Bethany worship team for a year playing bass guitar.

Being new in the country, I did not know how to start a church in this setting. How do I connect with people? How do I meet them? I had to innovate to reach my target audience. I tried various ways, like going to the mall to find those whom I wanted to reach. I learned that some Filipinos gathered at the mall on Saturday mornings to walk together. They also brought coffee and food so they could spend time with one another.

"Phone's for You"

Then I learned about "Phone's for You." This was a program that worked before cell phones became popular. Most people relied on their telephones at home or land lines. The basic strategy was to get a phone book, separate certain portions of the city and look for Filipino-sounding names. It was a tedious job. Using a street directory, we sectioned off westside Long Beach, listing down Filipino-sounding surnames. We rented a room and eight telephone lines for my small team from my weekly home Bible class.

Every night for six weeks, we made calls, beginning with, "Good evening. Have I reached a Filipino home?" and went on to share that we were offering to have small home Bible study groups and if they would be interested in coming.

At the end of six weeks, we had made around 18,000 calls—6,000 were Filipinos, the rest were Hispanic. Out of 6,000 around 2,000 were receptive to our message. We then invited the 2,000 to a free concert featuring a young singing group that was quite well-known in the Philippines. Out of the 2,000 invited, 600 said yes, but only 200 came to the concert. We announced during the event that we were starting a new church and invited them to come to the first service the following Sunday. About 50 came, and they became the core of the new church.

One of our first "Phone's for You" contacts was a lady and her mother. Joy Galazo, one of our callers, received a positive response from them. That lady came to church, brought her family, and to this day is part of what eventually became Fil-Am Christian Fellowship. Not only did her immediate family join us, but also several brothers, sisters, in-laws, nephews, and nieces became part of Fil-Am, serving as Sunday School teachers, worship team members, youth leaders, and officers, working in various capacities. That family was Joy's legacy, as she entered her reward when she passed away on August 29, 2011.

Evangelistic Outreaches

Early on, our new church now called Fil-Am Christian Fellowship continued to be engaged in different evangelistic outreaches such as concerts, one-on-one evangelism, and training of our members in various ministry skills.

To put our new church on the map, we sponsored the Manila Children's Choir headed by Dr. Lucresia Kasilag, National Artist, and former president of the

Manila Children's Choir

Cultural Center of the Philippines. We placed the 30-plus children and their chaperones in the homes of our members. We held the concert at Bethany Church and around 800 people came to watch, mostly Filipinos.

We also sponsored Eddie Mesa and his son, Mark Gil, Ray-an Fuentes, Marilen Martinez, Lirio Vital, Cecile Azarcon, and the singing group, Seven, who were all known in the Filipino community. We even invited other Christian celebrities like Fred Galang, an award winning actor, and Francis Arnaiz, a retired professional basketball player, to visit our church and share their testimonies. Several people who heard the Gospel at the presentations decided to receive Christ and some became part of our church.

EE Training

Our Evangelism Explosion (EE) training also resulted in the conversion of several people, notably a couple whom we visited in their home as part of our on-the-job training or OJT. The team was composed of five people: Cora Flores, Jane Galazo, Gener Jacinto, Lynn, and me. The couple invited us to come in, and we requested to talk to each of them separately. We found out that the wife had previously received Christ when she was in college but was not very involved in church. The husband, when asked if he was sure of going to heaven if he were to die that night, responded, "I've traveled around the world serving in the Navy for over 20 years, and no one has ever asked me that question."

After hearing the presentation, he prayed to receive Christ. The couple became part of the church and served in various capacities. Their names: Angelito and Loida Cadiente.

Years later, the Cadientes took the EE training and joined us in visiting another family for their OJT—a family of five. That night, Mr. and Mrs. Tony Aranas and their three grown children—Blessie, Belinda, and Anthony—all accepted Christ. We held a weekly Bible study in their home for over a year. We used the basic follow-up materials from EE, and later the *Experiencing God* study series.

Growing Pains

While the church continued to grow numerically, we were also concerned about the spiritual growth of those within. One of our church leaders confessed about his unresolved moral issue, a secret that he had kept for many years. When I learned about it, I set the motion for a disciplinary process with the goal of restoration. The people who were chosen to be members of the restoration committee were those trusted by the person to be disciplined, church leaders with whom he was comfortable. This brother gave me permission to use his real name, since, according to him, "It's in the past."

After several months of meeting with him weekly, the committee unanimously recommended to the church board that our brother Romy be fully restored. We set aside a date for a restoration service. At the service, we announced in front of the whole congregation that having met all requirements, our brother who fell can now be fully restored. He came to the stage and shared his testimony, thanking the committee and the church for their support, understanding, and forgiveness. After we prayed for him, I then handed him a Certificate of Restoration, signed by members of the committee. The people formed a line on either side of the aisle. Then he and his wife walked in the middle as everyone extended to him the right hand of fellowship. What a beautiful picture of forgiveness and full acceptance! It was a day of rejoicing!

Through the years, my relationship with Angelito and Romy grew and developed. They started out as mere contacts, then they became church members, and eventually active leaders. They both served as chairman of the board of elders at different times. Now they are my close friends, colleagues, and co-workers. To this day, I treasure their friendship.

A House of Worship

Our group started to meet in a Sunday School room of Bethany Church called "The ARC." Later, the space became too small for us, so we got permission to use the church gym for our services, however, we did not stay there long because the acoustics were not good. We searched for another venue, and we found an old church building on 3rd and Obispo Streets, near downtown Long Beach. It was owned by a dying church that needed renters. We worshiped at the Obispo location for a few years, then I learned that a CB church at Wrigley Heights in west Long Beach was about to close because of decreasing attendance.

At about this time, Rev. John Redman, who used to be the pulpit minister in my home church in the

Philippines, CCBC, while serving as a missionary with FEBC recently became the Executive Director of CB Southern California. He knew about the church at Wrigley Heights and contacted me, asking if I would like Fil-Am to have a building of its own. Of course, I would! I just didn't know how much it would cost us. The church property, which also included a pastoral house, was valued at 1.2 million dollars at that time. Fil-Am did not have the money. CB offered the property to us for $250,000, almost one million less than its current value. Fil-Am decided to buy the property. CB Southern California did not only sell the property for a ridiculously low amount, but they also changed the roof, removed the asbestos in the Sunday School building, and cut down a termite-infested tree in front of the pastoral house. That was another surprise!

When we moved to Wrigley Heights, the remaining members of the old church, a handful of elderly Americans and a few Hispanics, joined us. Instantly, Fil-Am became multicultural! We occupied the facility in June of 1997, less than 10 years from the time we started. When I accepted the challenge to plant a church, remember that I made a commitment to stay with the church until it got its own property, and I did.

Church Planting Director

Three months after we moved to our new location, I received a call from Rev. John Redman, inviting me to lunch to discuss some important matters. I thought CBSC was going to increase the price of the church property. Instead, at that meeting, Redman extended an offer to me to become the director of Church Planting of CBSC. He said to take my time and pray about it. I did accept the position and agreed to start the beginning of the new year.

I stayed with the association for almost five years. Several churches were started during my stewardship, including another Filipino church, two Hispanic churches, and a couple of Caucasian churches.

A Turn-Around Church

Around that time, the financial crisis in California happened, the housing bubble burst, and most organizations were affected, including CBSC. They had to downsize the staff, and I was one of those who was laid off. About the same time, a small Filipino Church in the city of Arcadia just lost its pastor and was looking for someone to take his place. My co-worker, Tony Pezzotta, told me about the plight of the struggling church in Arcadia.

One day a man named George Orejudos called. He introduced himself as the chairman of the board of elders of Christian Bible Fellowship (CBF) in Arcadia. He asked if I would visit the church. Since the invitation was to "visit," I was amenable to it. When I went, I met 15 discouraged people. After the service, the leaders asked me if I would consider accepting the responsibility of pastoring the church.

I proposed instead that I could serve as interim pastor. The idea was to have a testing period of six months to get to know each other better. After that, I could help them plan their next move. In the meantime, those who left the church gradually started to return when they learned that a new pastor was in town.

When the six-month testing time was over, the elders invited me to serve as the pastor. After praying about it, I accepted their invitation.

Remember Frank Obien who recruited me to join Campus Crusade 38 years before? We crossed paths again and I challenged him to serve as Worship Pastor at CBF, and he accepted. Moreover, I also challenged Jem Mendoza, an elder of the church, to become the Administrative Pastor. We became the CBF pastoral team—Pastor Frank Obien, Pastor Jem Mendoza, and I.

In 1968, Frank's father, Dr. Ermie Obien, met the father of Jem, Pastor Bayani Mendoza, in the Philippines. Pastor Bayani was then pastor of an Alliance church in Quezon City. Dr. Ermie challenged Pastor Bayani to work among Filipinos in the U.S. and he agreed. Soon after they arrived, Pastor Bayani and Mrs. Mendoza started home Bible classes that eventually became CBF. After all these years, God brought us together, so truly the CBF ministry had come full circle.

The first baptism at CBF after I became the pastor

During my tenure as pastor of CBF, we experienced growth not only numerically but also spiritually. We held several baptisms. We revived the summer camp. We worked with other churches to hold joint family camps at various locations. We met for days of prayer and retreats and sponsored several musical evangelistic concerts featuring

Filipino artists. For a couple of years, we held special classes for members like, how to study the Bible, how to preach, and how to lead Bible studies, to name a few. We sponsored a couple of Evangelism Explosion (EE) Training sessions. We also participated in medical missions. At one point, I led several members on a vision trip to Thailand and a neighboring country.

As I was carrying these responsibilities, age was catching up with me. I was 71 years old. I informed the elders that I planned to retire at 72. I gave the church almost a year to look for someone to take my place. December 14, 2014, was my last Sunday as CBF pastor.

I thought that was the end of my active ministry, but God had another plan. Yes, I retired from the pastorate but obviously I was not retiring from doing ministry. God had other plans.

GOING BACK TO SCHOOL

During my time with Campus Crusade, staff members were not allowed to go to school. The reason given was, since we were in the pioneering stage of the Philippine organization, we must give our full attention and energy to the work. We needed to concentrate on growing the ministry.

When I became Executive Director of CBAP, I found myself in a similar situation. I wanted to go to school but I couldn't, not because it was not allowed, but because of my responsibilities. Not only was I leading the association, but I was also traveling a lot, visiting churches, and surveying various provinces for church planting possibilities. Besides, I was really enjoying my work.

Desire to Study

My desire for further education was rekindled when I became a member of the board of trustees of FEBIAS College of Bible and Asian Theological Seminary (ATS). I also realized that I was always giving and investing in others but did not have much time for self-improvement. I felt that I was getting emptier inside. I needed to refresh and sharpen myself. I knew I needed to do something. I was also getting older.

When I reached 40, I enrolled at ATS part time, taking one or two subjects that I enjoyed. One of the faculty members talked to me and said, "Because of your 20 years of experience in the ministry, we would like you to consider taking validation exams on different courses of your choice to prove that you know the subjects. We'll give you a grade accordingly." I accepted the offer and completed the Master of Divinity requirements in 18 months instead of 3 years.

Because of my involvement in evangelism, church planting, and church growth, I focused on learning more about missions. I asked some of my teachers and others in the know about what school I should look at. They suggested several schools. I decided on enrolling at Fuller School of World Mission (now called School of Intercultural Studies) in Pasadena, California, because the school offered courses that interested me most.

Fuller School of World Mission

At Fuller, I was under some of the best minds in missions including Dr. Paul Hiebert, (Urban Studies, Cultural Anthropology), Dr. C. Peter Wagner (Church Growth), Dr. Dan Shaw and Dr. Charles Kraft (Cultural Anthropology and Communication), Dr. Robert "Bobby" Clinton (Leadership), and Dr. Charles "Chuck" Van Engen (Theology of Missions), among others. Dr. Van Engen served as my mentor and personal advisor. Occasionally, he asked me to teach his class for him whenever he had emergencies.

By the way, what impressed me about most of my Fuller professors was the fact that they were former missionaries. I appreciated the insights that they learned from the mission field. They were not just academics but also practitioners. They knew what they were talking about both from experience and education.

After finishing my Master of Theology (Th.M.) degree, I had to take a comprehensive exam to be admitted to the PhD program. I don't know how I did it, but miracle of miracles, I passed.

My dissertation proposal was approved by the doctoral committee, and so I was on my way to continue my education on the next level. While studying full time, I was also pastoring the church that I started three years earlier in Long Beach. Three times a week, I commuted between Long Beach and Pasadena which was at least 45 minutes each way.

As per requirement, I had to read 50 books (or an equivalent of 10,000 pages) on missions for my Literature Survey course and write a one-page review on each book. This had to be done within one quarter or 10 weeks. At this stage, classroom sessions were limited to seminars where we critiqued each other's papers that we were working on. I presented a paper for the Cultural Anthropology course about the activities of Filipino immigrants going to a fish market at San Pedro port every Saturday morning. My paper was titled, "It's a Fishy World."

As I look back, my Fuller days widened my horizon, deepened my theological core beliefs, and exposed me to diverse methods that worked in other parts of the world. I valued my exposure to church leaders from other countries. I had meaningful times of interaction with them. We had the same struggles in doing ministry. We were not alone.

Now I understand why the Lord delayed my going back to school. He allowed me to do ministry first so that I was able to understand and appreciate more what I was learning.

While I enjoyed studying, I was also working full time growing the church that I started. I had to make a choice which one should take more of my attention. I chose the ministry, thinking that I could go back to my studies later. Unfortunately, it did not happen. How I wish I could have done both.

Fuller graduation

MISSION TRIPS

During my time at CBF, I put emphasis on not just growing the church, but also on getting more involved in missions, both locally and globally. I led a team twice for vision casting in some Asian countries. These trips were held in coordination with a mission agency that focuses on reaching the ARNA (Access Restricted Nations of Asia). With me on that first trip were team members from CBF: George and Ella Orejudos, Col. and Mrs. Reuben Primavera, Mrs. Roming Hilario, Willy and Rose Tecson, Ed Wu, and Jem Mendoza.

Smuggling Bibles

The highlight of that trip was when we brought Bibles into one of those countries. Each of us was given a carry-on bag filled with Bibles in the language of the local people, a total of 280 copies in all.

The night before we left, we had a long prayer session. We were given instructions that should one of us get caught by Customs and Immigration

Praying over the Bibles for ARNA the night before the trip

officers, we were not to talk to any of the team members. We were to stay calm while in line, and to pretend that we did not know each other.

The following day, we took an hour and a half flight to the country of our destination. At the airport we were a solemn-looking bunch, silently praying that God would perform a miracle, that none of us would get caught. We were informed that anyone caught bringing Bibles into the country would be put in prison if they were locals. Foreigners would be interrogated, immediately deported, and subsequently blacklisted. The Bibles would be confiscated.

Another instruction was that once we got out of the airport, a group would be waiting for us, silently identified by our escort. We were to hand them the bags containing Bibles without saying a word.

While in line at Immigration, we saw a group of men about double our number standing in front of us. They all had shaved heads and wore long orange robes. The immigration officer just waved them in, and because we were behind them, we were also just let in. They didn't bother to inspect our luggage or ask us any questions. When they saw our American passports, they were very accommodating to us. We simply silently thanked the Lord with a collective sigh of relief. Another surprise.

The next time I saw those Bibles was in a meeting of pastors and church leaders in a church. The group requested me to turn over those Bibles symbolically to the head of the evangelical association of the country.

We all realized the importance of what we did when we went on tour and visited the Bible society office. We saw Bibles printed within the country that were approved by the government. Those were the only Bibles allowed to be distributed, that according to the local pastors, were not translated accurately and had some omissions. The Bibles, therefore, that we brought in were very precious to believers.

Turning over the smuggled Bibles

Co-Workers

On the Sunday of our visit, I spoke at a church located on the fifth floor of a high-rise building with no elevator. Our group was mostly composed of seniors. We walked up slowly. I don't remember how long it took us to reach the meeting place. I was surprised to learn that my interpreter was a lady who graduated from ATS, where I also studied. I was glad to know that ATS graduates in the country were faithfully serving the Lord in various capacities in different places.

Our guide and driver while we were in that country was on the staff of a mission agency. He shared with us that his eldest daughter was getting ready to attend college, but he did not have enough funds to pay for it. When we learned about it, our group decided to help put her through school. We committed to share $100 a month ($10 per person) for the next four years until she finished her course. The last time we heard, the girl had graduated and was working as an executive of a prestigious car company in Bangkok.

Back to ARNA

The next time I went back to an ARNA was with my son, Jay. Our team consisted of the two of us plus my cousin, Susan, a missionary in Thailand. We flew from Bangkok to the nearest border of the country of our destination. Again, we carried Bibles and safely brought them in.

After we traveled on a 10-kilometer "no man's land" in a Volvo with a Toyota engine that had seen better days, we met with some pastors. They gladly accepted the Bibles that we brought. Later, we visited a house church. I gave the message through an interpreter. Then we went to the villages and met some more believers. A woman who had cancer requested prayer, and Jay prayed for her.

On a different occasion, I spoke at another house church where people sat on the floor during the worship service. The singing was accompanied by a guitar and an indigenous instrument. After the service, we went to a nearby fishpond farm and had a picnic lunch. We had tilapia and a native delicacy made of fried frog.

With my cousin Susan and son Jay

At another place, Susan showed us a well which 300 people depended on for their water supply.

The problem was, during the summer months, the well went dry. I asked how much it would cost to put a pump. "About $1,000 to buy the materials" was the answer given. The people would provide labor. When I returned to CBF, I shared this need with the members and several pitched in to help. We were able to send the money, and the village got their more constant water supply.

The two mission trips made a deep impression on me as I observed the faithfulness of the Christians amid restrictions and difficulty. They were persecuted, lacked resources, and the leaders needed ministerial training. The Bibles were scarce, hence the need to smuggle Bibles from the outside. We must really uphold in prayer our brothers and sisters in these Access Restricted Nations of Asia.

JARS

JARS was officially organized in 2004 in Big Bear, California. It started out as my personal vision which I shared with a few colleagues who had a heart for ministry. These men and women were at a family camp with me that week, so we sat together and brainstormed about the organization that became known as JARS.

Philosophy Behind

Originally, JARS didn't stand for anything. It was simply "Jars," an ordinary container made of dried clay used for fetching water. The vision is based on II Corinthians 4:7, which says, *"But we have this treasure in jars of clay to show that this all-surpassing power is from God and not from us."*

The general idea is to be able to assist Christian workers ("jars of clay") in several ways, especially those laboring in rural areas. We wanted to encourage them in any way we can. Many pastors in the provinces are not financially stable. Churches can not support them sufficiently, yet they are so faithful, remaining in the ministry, often at a great sacrifice.

Scholarships

One of the things that JARS does is help pastors' kids with their college education. Those pastors who are receiving below P10,000 ($200.00) a month are qualified to apply for a scholarship for one of their children. The idea was to put the kid through school, taking care of tuition and books, and after graduating, they could, in turn, support their other siblings. One main qualification is that at least one of the parents is in full-time ministry. The student must maintain a passing grade and submit the grade at the end of each year until they finish their baccalaureate degree. Before the pandemic, JARS had already graduated 14 individuals, including teachers, engineers, a veterinarian, and nurses, among others.

Medical Mission

The other big project that JARS (now stands for Jesus' Ambassadors Ready to Serve) undertakes is the Medical Mission, which focuses on helping needy communities in the provinces. Over the years, we have been working in cooperation with Operation Compassion of Greenhills Christian Fellowship (GCF), who provide medical professionals like doctors, dentists, and nurses. We've also worked with volunteers from different local churches. We usually work with a local church or a church planter that helps with witnessing, counseling, and follow-up after the medical mission is over. We also raise funds to buy medicines and other supplies.

The first Medical Mission was held in Laoag City where we reached out to several *barangays* (villages), inviting the people to come for medical examination, dental treatment, and free medication. We rented a building

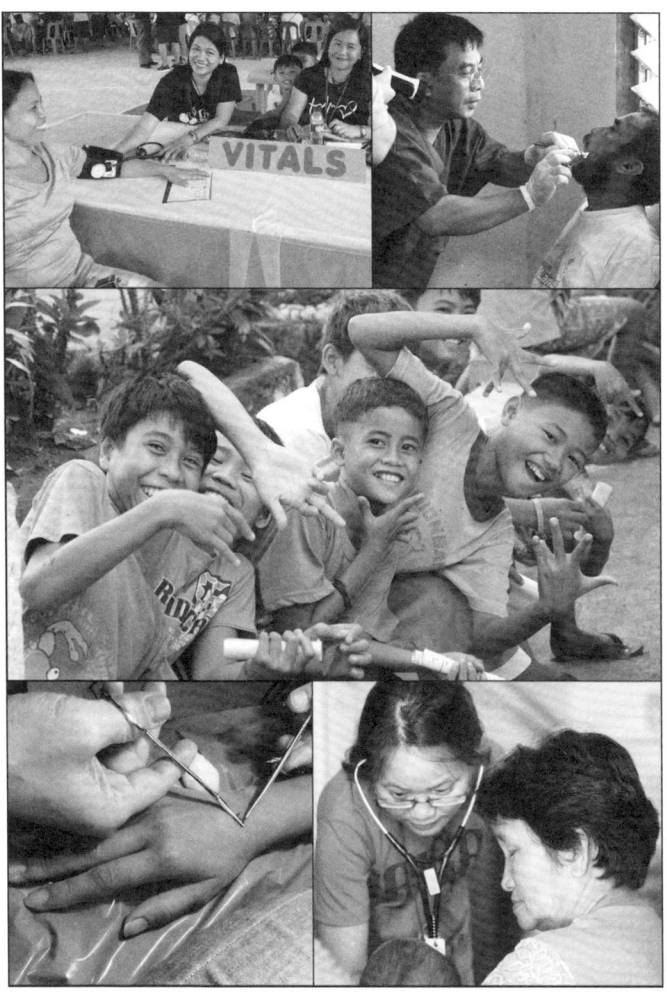

near City Hall. We invited city officials for a breakfast meeting and introduced ourselves and our reason for being there. When the city administrator learned that we were renting a hall, she said, "Since you are helping our community, you may use the facility for free. We are refunding your deposit." The city also sent health workers from the community centers and clinics to help us daily.

Volunteers from the U.S. and from local churches worked together to make the medical mission run smoothly. A group went to the venue at the crack of dawn to set up—arranging chairs and setting parameters for each station. People started coming as early as 6:00 in the morning, even though the announced opening was not until 8:00.

Their first stop was Registration and Vital Signs. Then they moved to Counseling where volunteers from our team and the churches interviewed them, shared Christ with them, and directed them to their next stop, like Medical (general check-ups, pediatrics, or minor surgery, meaning simple procedures like cysts or circumcision), Dental, or Optometry. The patients' last stop was Pharmacy, where they received free vitamins, and medication prescribed by the doctors or dentists.

Working from morning till late afternoon, our team of health care professionals and other volunteers were exhausted but happy to be able to serve the people. These doctors and dentists were on the staff of hospitals or had their own practice in Manila, but they donated their time to share the love of God through their expertise. After two consecutive summers in Laoag, JARS Medical Mission has brought us to

other places like Hermosa, Bataan; Iba and Botolan, Zambales; Iriga, Camarines Sur; Bacolod, Talisay, and Magalona in Negros Occidental (where two churches were started as a result of the mission); San Jose, Occidental Mindoro; General Santos, Sarangani; Sariaya, Quezon; and Odiongan and Looc, Romblon.

Our ride in Iba & Botolan, Zambales

We set up a ten-fold goal for our the Medical Mission, namely:
1. Provide appropriate treatment to everyone who comes.
2. Communicate the message of love and forgiveness.
3. Lead the interested ones to receive the free gift of God.
4. Connect contacts with the local church leadership.
5. Connect with city officials from all levels.

6. Connect with the city's businesses and educational leaders.
7. Encourage the local congregation in every way possible.
8. Turn over contacts to the local church leadership.
9. Create a sustainable program for the local ministry to grow.
10. Set up a workable structure to maintain the growth of the church.

Future of JARS

Because of the pandemic, most of JARS' projects were put on hold. At this writing, the U.S. and the Philippine Board of Trustees of JARS are making plans to resume its ministry projects. I am just thankful that the Lord has used JARS so far. I have since turned over the helm of JARS to younger leaders. I am confident that as the new personnel continue the work, JARS will be a strong partner of the church.

MY SIBLINGS

The union of Estanislao Baldemor and Dionisia Cainto produced seven children: Dolores, Rogelio, Oscar (me), Clarita, Nelia, Jean, who passed away at age six, and Wilson. Of the six who remained, the three girls became school teachers while the three boys went into the ministry.

Dolores (Dols), the eldest, finished her Elementary Education course at a young age, and immediately started teaching at Paete Elementary School. Her co-teachers soon noticed her intelligence, leadership skills, and honesty. Parents, pupils, and co-teachers looked up to her and often sought her advice and her wise counsel.

When she became a Christian, she emerged as one of the leaders at our home church. She became an effective witness especially to her co-workers. She taught Bible classes to all ages including women, youth, and some families. She organized and led an early morning daily prayer meeting composed of mostly adult women. The members of NTBC in Paete today trace the church's growth and success to the faithfulness of those dawn prayer warriors.

Regrettably, my eldest sister died young, succumbing to cancer two-weeks before her 50th birthday.

Rogelio (Roger), my older brother whom I called Kuya, held the distinction of being the first convert of missionaries in my hometown. He accepted the Lord at an after-school Bible class held at our local high school. A serious student, Roger excelled in school. He soon decided that he wanted to be a pastor and enrolled in Bible school with the help and encouragement of the missionaries and our parents. He pastored NTBC and Lucena Baptist Church, where he served for over 12 years. He was the first ordained CB pastor. During the early days of the CB movement in our country, they produced a movie called, "Heart of the Philippines," which told the story of Roger's life.

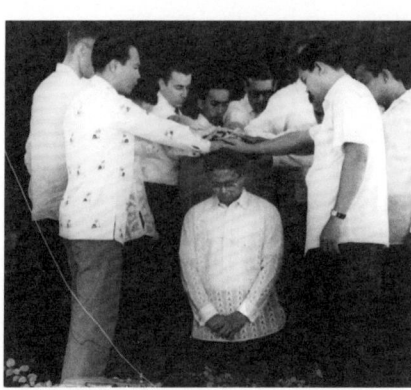
Kuya Roger's ordination

I admired my Kuya and followed in his footsteps in going to Bible school. We later worked together both in Campus Crusade where he led the "I FOUND IT!" campaign and at CBAP where he became Director of Church Development. Kuya Roger died young in 1994, but his influence lives on through those whom he had ministered to.

Clarita (Claire), the sibling immediately after me, is quite outgoing. When I was barely three years old, and the center of attention in our family. I was hostile to her. I was asleep when she was born. When I woke up, I found her next to my mother and I was not the baby anymore. I begged my mother to return this "stranger" back to the midwife who assisted her during her delivery. Sibling rivalry, however, did not last long. We eventually got along.

As she grew up, she manifested a passion for oration and declamation both in the vernacular and in English. This talent gave her the prestige of delivering poetic honors to town fiesta queens in our hometown and other celebrations.

Claire graduated from one of the distinguished learning institutes in the country, the Philippine Normal College. She taught at the International Christian Academy and Grace Christian Academy where she worked with professional people with the same faith and relationship with the Lord.

When she moved to Guam, she accepted a position at a private school managed by men and women in uniform—the U.S. Navy. She retired in 2021.

Nelia (Neyah) was much younger than me, but we had some good times together when she lived with us in Quezon City while she was in college. She was with us when our eldest son, Timothy Carl, had the accident that took his life. She became close to our family, especially with our little daughter, Celine (formerly nicknamed Chinky).

Neyah told us how she gave a copy of the Four Spiritual Laws booklet to a new acquaintance, Eddie, who prayed to receive Christ. The two of them became friends and later fell in love. When they got married, guess who was a flower girl? Chinky, of course.

Neyah and Eddie made their home in Batangas. At the same time, Eddie received the call to serve the Lord.

He finished his seminary training while serving as pastor of Tanauan Bible Church.

The Lord blessed his ministry tremendously and the church gave birth to several daughter churches. Nelia embraced her role as pastor's wife while at the same time pursuing a career as a school teacher. She went on to further her education, eventually earning the Doctor of Education (Ed. D) degree while working as Regional Supervisor at the Department of Education.

After Neyah retired, she later became ill. She bravely battled her disease but a few years later, after marking their golden anniversary as a couple, she went home to be with the Lord on April 29, 2023. While so sad over the death of my youngest sister, I considered it a unique privilege to speak at her funeral. There I met scores of people who were touched by her life and influence, many of them a result of that initial incident of sharing Christ with her friend who became her future husband.

My youngest sibling, **Wilson (Wil)**, is the quiet one. He is a meticulous electronics technician who also answered the call to Christian service. He studied at a Bible school and later served as pastor in several places including Cabanatuan City, Candelaria, Pagsanjan, Paete, and Los Baños. He is a deep thinker and a good preacher.

In 2002, he and his wife, Cel, a nurse, immigrated to Wales in the United Kingdom. Four years ago, Wilson lost his wife to cancer.

Out of the six siblings, three are now in the presence of Jesus. Three of us are living in different parts of the world: Philippines, U.K., and U.S.A. We seldom see each other but the love we share continues to inspire us to keep the communication lines open and to pray for each other.

OUR GROWING TRIBE

There were six of us when we left the Philippines more than three decades ago. We had two teenagers and two elementary school age kids. As of this writing our tribe has grown to 14. Added were two in-laws and six grandchildren. Let me introduce them to you.

Cecilia Ann or **Celine,** our eldest daughter, currently works at Novo, a missions agency (formerly called Church Resource Ministries or CRM). She completed her bachelor's degree in World Arts and Cultures from University of California at Los Angeles (UCLA) and also finished graduate studies in Ethnomusicology at the same school. She also has a degree in Graphic

Communication and works as a graphic designer and production coordinator. Celine is involved at her church and serves as board secretary with JARS Ministries. She also volunteers for GLOW (God's Love on Wheels), a wheelchair distribution ministry. She enjoys traveling and likes visiting interesting and beautiful places with her friends. She has been to several countries including Spain, Mexico, Canada, Japan, Vietnam, Venezuela, Hungary, and Austria.

Our only son, **Jonathan Carl** or **Jay**, for short, worked in sales at different companies, as previously mentioned, then with Yahoo, after which he ventured into starting his own business. Later, he sold his first business and formed Gruv Gear, a company that produces and distributes innovative musician's paraphernalia, designed mostly by Jay himself. Gruv Gear products are sold in over 55 countries all over the world. He is married to **Janeth**, who left her nursing career after 18 years to help her husband in the company, where she serves as vice president. They have two grown sons: **Jyrus Creed**, an aspiring actor, and **Jyles Caelen**, who is following in his dad's footsteps as a businessman. Jay and his family are actively serving at their church.

Lynette Faith, our second daughter, graduated from California State University at Fullerton with a BA in English and an MS in Literacy and Reading Education. A professor at Long Beach City College, she is also a homeschool teacher to her two youngest children. She volunteers with JARS Ministries in her spare time.

Lynette is married to **Kevin Akio Tolentino**, who has been working for the U.S. Postal Service for the past 24 years and also recently became a longshoreman. Kevin is Filipino-Japanese, hence their four children's Japanese middle names.

Saige Katana, an 11th grader, is on her school's golf team. She loves to cook pasta and has a talent for baking and designing pastries. She enjoys photography and is a member of the photography club at school. She wants to pursue a career either in photography or marine biology. **Tallon Takeo** is in the ninth grade and plays soccer for his school and continues to be a valuable player for the same club soccer team he has been a part of for four years. He is a member of the school band, playing saxophone. He also plays the piano and is learning the guitar. **Reese Miyako**, who is in seventh grade, is a budding artist and dabbles in different art media. She has a heart for animals and takes very good care of her pet bunny. Reese is also an avid reader. The youngest, **Qai Kiyoshi**, is a fifth grader who is very creative and shoots videos of his soccer moves. He loves parkour, electronics, soccer, physical exercise, dogs, science TV shows, and food.

All four kids—Saige, Tallon, Reese, and Qai—achieve academic excellence each school year. They also got to participate in a weekend medical outreach in Sariaya, Quezon, in 2015.

Our youngest daughter is **Claudette Joyce**, whom we call **Odette**. She was in tourism for 15 years, much of that time serving as Membership Director at the Long Beach Convention and Visitors Bureau.

Two years after the pandemic, the Garden Grove Chamber of Commerce invited her as its President and CEO. She has been in that position for over a year, working closely with the city officials and local business owners. Odette's pride and joy are her two yellow Labradors, Onyx and Jasper, who are part of our family. They take walks twice a day and sleep in her room.

Odette currently serves as JARS Ministries' Chief Operating Officer. She has been very involved in its medical missions and other projects.

I thank God for our children. I'm very proud of them and their accomplishments. Busy as we all are, we try as a family to celebrate birthdays and most holidays together.

Our tribe has truly grown!

Front row: Jyles, Lynn, Oscar, Saige. Middle row: Janeth, Celine, Qai, Reese, Claudette, Lynette. Back row: Jay, Jyrus, Tallon, Kevin.

PEOPLE WHO INFLUENCED ME

Kuya Roger

The first influence in my life was Kuya Roger. When we were small, our father used to take us to work, to his farm up in the mountains. My brother was two-and-a-half years older than me, and he always helped me with the task assigned by our father, especially when I had to carry heavy loads like coconuts, lanzones, and bunches of bananas. He showed me how to balance the load to make it easier for me to carry them down the mountain trails. I followed him around. Even in playing boys' games, he was always the leader.
When he became a Christian, I continued to look up to him for direction. He was my model in the early years of my Christian life. We prayed together and on a few occasions we traveled together. I served as best man at his wedding, and he was mine.

What I learned from him was his seriousness in his studies. I also admired him for his speaking ability. He was a good preacher and an excellent debater.

Dr. William Simons

"Dad" Simons, as we younger co-workers used to call him, was a great influence in my life. He shared the Gospel with my family. He baptized me when I was 14. He officiated my wedding.

He was low-key but at the same time he knew what he wanted to accomplish. The mission work in Laguna province in the early days would not have flourished had it not been for his determination, faithfulness, and patience. Those of us who were familiar with his ministry would agree that he was a diligent and dedicated servant of God. He immersed himself in the culture and the community around him which resulted in the conversion of several of his neighbors.

Dad and Mom Simons' home was always open to everyone. I enjoyed staying there when I was a student and later with my family on several occasions. They made people feel important. Dad was a guy whom you could approach anytime. He always had time for me.

His humility especially impressed me. As a missionary, Dad Simons prepared us nationals to become leaders. When we did assume the leadership, he willingly worked with us. When I became General Director of CBAP, he served on the staff as Church Development Director. Years after he retired, he was invited to come back as President of ATS. At that time, I was Chairman of the ATS Board of Trustees. Once again, he showed his humble attitude by conferring with me on several important decisions.

Bishop Fred Magbanua

Fred Magbanua, whom I called "*Manong* (older brother) Fred," was a strong leader. Wherever you placed him, he would always emerge as the leader of the group, and yet he was willing to include younger workers like me to learn from him. It was my privilege to work under him for a year and a half as an intern at CCBC. He was the President of CBAP while I was serving as General Director, so we had an opportunity to work closely together again. He was a dedicated servant of the Lord. Over the years, he served as a pastor in the province, an engineer, and later, Managing Director of FEBC, a pastor at CCBC, and head of his own organization, Jesus Our Lord (JOL).

A humble man, he accepted criticism without getting mad. A diligent worker, he was willing to do almost anything. He was always learning from books, experience, and other people.

Manong Fred was kind and accommodating. One time I requested him to help me get an appointment with Bishop Emerito Nacpil of the United Methodist Church for a paper that I was doing. He not only made the appointment, but he also accompanied me to interview the good bishop.

When he was hospitalized at the National Kidney and Transplant Institute, I happened to be in Manila, and I visited him. He was in pain, but his sense of humor was still intact. He was joking around and reminiscing about our CCBC days. Little did I know that that was the last time I would see him. He went home to be with the Lord on January 21, 2013.

Jake Toews

I worked closely with Jake for many years. He was my Associate Director, but our working relationship was as equals. We had memorable times traveling together, visiting churches, strategizing, advising, and counseling church planters. He was generous to a fault, specifically to the church planters with whom he worked. Another thing that I noticed was how he identified himself with national workers—sleeping in huts with them, eating what they ate, and spending time with them. He loved the Filipinos.

He was willing to do anything that we asked him to do. He diligently did his tasks without fanfare. Jake Toews was a great example of a servant leader. He played a major part in the success and fulfillment of O-200 and Harvest 20,000.

I treasured his keen observation, his advice, and helpful suggestions. We became very close, and he requested that I do his funeral when the time came. I flew from Los Angeles to Minnesota in September 2004 to fulfill his request.

Ricardo B. Jumawan

RBJ, as he was commonly called in our circle, had a great impact both on my personal and professional life. Since I met him, he had become an inspiration, a counselor, an adviser, a colleague, and most of all a friend—all rolled into one. I count it a real privilege to personally learn from him.

Ric was not an armchair leader; he always got involved in the job. He did not mind rolling up his sleeves and getting his hands dirty to accomplish a given task. Whenever he wanted a job done, he gave his instructions in the form of a request, not a command.

When we were forming the Filipino CB Association of America, he used to drive from his place in Oakland to the Los Angeles area (371 miles or 576 km one way), lead the meeting for several hours, then drive back to Oakland the same night.

Ric was a beloved friend and co-worker who passed away in April 2021. I still miss him. I am what I am today largely because of the impact, impression, and influence RBJ had in my life.

WHAT THEN?

So many things have happened since we came to the U.S. 35 years ago. I went back to school, planted and pastored two churches, became an administrator again as Church Planting Director with CBSC, pastored a turn-around church that needed help, and founded a new organization. At the same time while doing all this, at the back of my mind, I would often think of the possibility of returning to the Philippines. This feeling visited me every time we went on a medical mission. I felt that while I had retired from the pastorate, I'm still not retired from ministry.

The question is not IF I'm going back, but WHEN? What will I do? And how do I live far away from my family, especially the grandchildren?

Before my 80th birthday, our four adult children presented us with a challenge. They reminded us that for years we have been talking about a ministry to pastors and Christian workers, a vision to help men and women who are serving the Lord. Many pastors in the provinces cannot afford to take a much needed rest. Taking some time off is a luxury. We would like to give an opportunity for them to get some rest and have a personal retreat at minimal expense to them—to rest their bodies and renew their spirits. When they go back home, refreshed and recharged, they'll be able to minister more effectively.

Our children have been aware of our dream to help pastors. They even came up with a name for the ministry—"Rest, Renew, Restore". They challenged us to start the new ministry and to set it up in the Philippines and begin the ball rolling at the soonest possible time. Our children said they're willing to partner with us.

To begin with, we will invite a couple or two for a three-day relaxation (physical) and personal retreat (spiritual). In the process of resting, they will be renewed. They will have a simple guide on how to do a personal retreat—it will be semi-structured —so when they return to their ministry, they will have been refreshed and recharged.

In March of this year (2023), we experimented to see how our plan will work. We invited a couple to take three days away from their work. We requested some people to assist them with whatever they needed and talk to them informally about themselves and their ministry. The couple went home, grateful for the time to rest. When I visited him at his church a few weeks later, I gave him the book, *Ordering Your Private World* by Gordon Macdonald.

So, this seems to be the direction that we are taking at our age. We will most likely stay in the Philippines for a few months, share the vision of "Rest, Renew, Restore" with potential partners and volunteers and see how God will lead to make this vision a reality. We are making it a matter of prayer. We would like to invite you—the reader—to partner with us in prayer.

*However, I consider my life worth nothing to me; my only aim is to finish the race and complete the task the Lord Jesus has given me—***the task of testifying to the good news of God's grace.*** (Acts 20:24)

Soli Deo Gloria (Glory to God Alone)